"Twant me, 'twas the Lord. I always told Him, 'I trust to You. I don't know where to go or what to do, but I expect You to lead me,' and He always did."
—Harriet Tubman

Sweet Carolina MYSTERIES

Roots and Wings
Picture-Perfect Mystery
Angels Watching Over Me
A Change of Art
Conscious Decisions
Surrounded by Mercy

Sweet Carolina MYSTERIES

SURROUNDED by MERCY

Elizabeth Penney

Sweet Carolina Mysteries is a trademark of Guideposts.

Published by Guideposts Books & Inspirational Media
100 Reserve Road, Suite E200
Danbury, CT 06810
Guideposts.org

Copyright © 2023 by Guideposts. All rights reserved.

This book, or parts thereof, may not be reproduced, stored in a retrieval system, or transmitted in any form or by any means, electronic, mechanical, photocopying, recording, or otherwise, without the written permission of the publisher.

This is a work of fiction. While the setting of Mercy Hospital as presented in this series is fictional, the location of Charleston, South Carolina, actually exists, and some places and characters may be based on actual places and people whose identities have been used with permission or fictionalized to protect their privacy. Apart from the actual people, events, and locales that figure into the fiction narrative, all other names, characters, businesses, and events are the creation of the author's imagination and any resemblance to actual persons or events is coincidental.

Every attempt has been made to credit the sources of copyrighted material used in this book. If any such acknowledgment has been inadvertently omitted or miscredited, receipt of such information would be appreciated.

Scripture references are from the following sources: *The Holy Bible, King James Version* (KJV). *The Holy Bible, New International Version* (NIV). Copyright ©1973, 1978, 1984, 2011 by Biblica, Inc. Used by permission of Zondervan. All rights reserved worldwide. www.zondervan.com

Cover and interior design by Müllerhaus
Cover illustration by Bob Kayganich at Illustration Online LLC.
Typeset by Aptara, Inc.

This book was previously published under the title *Surrounded by Mercy* as part of the *Miracles & Mysteries of Mercy Hospital* series.

Printed and bound in the United States of America
10 9 8 7 6 5 4 3 2 1

SURROUNDED
~~~ by ~~~
MERCY

Let them give thanks to the L ORD for his unfailing love
and his wonderful deeds for mankind,
for he satisfies the thirsty and
fills the hungry with good things.

Psalm 107:8–9 (NIV)

Chapter One

THE MORNING AIR WAS FRESH and sweet as Evelyn Perry strode along Logan Street toward Mercy Hospital, where she managed the records department. The calendar said November, but here in Charleston, South Carolina, flowers bloomed in gardens and window boxes, and birds chirped in the trees overhanging the street. Flocks of cheeky pigeons strutted about the sidewalk, as if eager for someone to toss them a snack.

"Not today, pigeons," Evelyn muttered, her mind on her ever-growing to-do list. Thanksgiving was only three weeks away, and this year she and her husband, James, were hosting several good friends and their families. Joy, Anne, and Shirley also worked at Mercy Hospital, and the foursome had become close while solving the mysteries and miracles swirling around the historic landmark hospital. Now, with the busy holidays looming, Evelyn quite frankly hoped for a break from all the excitement.

Evelyn's steps quickened as she passed through the hospital's tall wrought iron gates and headed toward the lobby entrance. She had just enough time for a quick cup of coffee and a chat with her friends before her Monday morning officially started.

But as the automatic doors shut behind her, she paused to appreciate the lobby, a daily ritual. Founded in the 1820s, Mercy Hospital was a beautiful blend of old-fashioned charm and up-to-the-minute patient care. The lobby's stained-glass windows, cypress wood paneling, and painted-sky ceiling created an elegant but welcoming ambiance for patients and employees alike. If not for the staff in scrubs bustling through, anyone might think this was the lobby of a grand hotel.

She loved working here, in the very heart of Charleston life. Almost everyone came through at one time or another, as patient or visitor.

With a sigh of satisfaction, Evelyn started moving in the direction of the gift shop, where she was meeting her friends.

"Good morning, Evelyn." Joy Atkins, the gift shop manager, greeted her with a big smile. "Coffee?" A recent widow and transplant to Charleston from Houston, Texas, Joy had transformed the gift shop into a welcoming space. Not only did the shop sell nice gifts and gorgeous floral arrangements—often supplemented by Joy's own flowers—but a fresh pot of coffee was always on.

"I'd love a cup." Evelyn set her handbag on the counter and unbuttoned her wool car coat. She loved to wear vintage brooches on her lapel, and today's choice featured acorns and oak leaves. "Have you seen Anne or Shirley yet?"

"Anne's here somewhere," Joy said as she hurried toward the coffee station in the back room. "And Shirley said she'd try to make it." Anne Mabry was a longtime volunteer at the hospital, and Shirley Bashore was a nurse, also new to Charleston. Shirley floated between departments, which meant her hours and assignments changed almost daily.

While she waited for her friend to return, Evelyn made a circuit of the shop, noting new items and admiring the colorful bouquets in the cooler, especially one featuring fluffy white hydrangeas and small pink roses. "Are those from your garden?" she asked Joy.

Joy's blue eyes sparkled as she handed Evelyn a mug of coffee. "Yes, ma'am. I brought in three and already sold two."

"I can see why." Evelyn laughed. "I wish I had someone to bless with that bouquet." She took a sip of dark, rich coffee, made with beans Joy ordered from Texas. "Not that I want anyone to be in the hospital, of course."

"Of course not," Joy said. "Though sometimes it's for a happy reason."

Evelyn smiled. "Having a baby, you mean." Mercy Hospital had a maternity ward and neonatal unit, and Evelyn loved viewing the new arrivals in the glass-fronted nursery. She and James had never been blessed with children, but she so enjoyed spoiling her friends' grandchildren and Mercy's young patients.

Joy glanced toward the shop door. "Speaking of which, I had a pregnant visitor stop in earlier, but she left when she saw I was busy. I hope she comes back."

"I love how conscientious you are," Evelyn said. Joy's quiet but caring nature had won many hearts at the hospital. She was also known for her offers to pray for the patients her customers were visiting.

Anne Mabry, the third member of their gang, entered the gift shop, her blond pageboy bouncing. "Hey, ladies. Lovely day, isn't it?" Anne's gift for hospitality made her a natural when it came to volunteering at the hospital. As a former pastor's wife, she was well able to deal with people of all personalities, even the difficult ones.

"It sure is," Evelyn said as Joy went to pour coffee for Anne. She pulled a small notebook out of her handbag. "I was hoping we could talk about the Thanksgiving menu today, figure out what everyone is bringing."

Anne clapped a hand to her forehead. "I can't believe it. Thanksgiving is right around the corner. My, how time flies."

"It sure seems to go faster the older I get," Joy said as she popped out of the back room, mug in hand. She handed the cup to Anne. "Put me down for green bean and sweet potato casseroles."

"And I'll bake pies, of course," Anne said. Her pecan pie was famous. "Pumpkin, pecan, and chocolate chess."

"Yum," Evelyn said as she made notes. "Both of you." She tapped her pen on the counter. "I'm making turkey with dressing and a huge pot of mashed potatoes. Plus I'll put out cheese and crackers and a veggie platter with dip for starters."

"You're doing a lot," Joy objected as she ran a dustcloth along a shelf. "What else can I bring?"

Evelyn pointed the pen at her. "Flowers. How about putting together a couple of arrangements for the table?" Her dining room table had leaves to make it longer, and she'd be using them.

"Love to," Joy said. She looked out into the lobby. "Here comes Shirley. I'll get her a cup of coffee."

Anne said, "I'll also bring apple cider and cokes."

"Perfect, Anne." Evelyn peered out the shop windows and saw the last member of their group approaching. Shirley was dressed in scrubs, and her dark, curly hair was pinned up out of the way.

"Finally," the nurse said with a sigh as she entered the gift shop. "The emergency room has been *crazy* today." She accepted the hot java from Joy with thanks and took a long sip.

"We've been talking about what everyone is making for our Thanksgiving dinner," Evelyn said. She read the list out loud.

"Put me down for corn casserole and Mama's biscuits," Shirley said. Her mother, Regina—the reason Shirley had relocated from Atlanta—made the best biscuits ever. Soft, flaky, and melt-in-your-mouth delicious.

"I sure will." Evelyn jotted down Shirley's items. "What a great menu. Thanks, everyone."

"And thank you for hosting," Shirley said. "Mama and I are looking forward to it." She took another swallow of coffee. "There's something else I wanted to talk to y'all about. Especially you, Evelyn." Once all eyes were expectantly upon her, Shirley went on. "A good friend of mine from church, Abigail Gibbs Johnson? She and her husband own Abigail's Kitchen."

Anne smiled. "That's one of the best restaurants in town."

"It sure is," Evelyn said. Abigail's Kitchen made fantastic buttermilk fried chicken paired with Southern sides like collard greens, macaroni and cheese, and fried okra.

Shirley's laugh was hearty as she put up a hand. "Hold on. Let me finish. This isn't about the restaurant. Well, it sort of is. Did you know that Abigail's great-great-great-grandmother founded the place back before the Civil War? The original Abigail Gibbs. She was married to a man named Israel." She paused dramatically. "He was either a scoundrel or a hero, depending upon your point of view."

Evelyn's pulse quickened. She loved uncovering stories from the past, learning more about former generations and the lives they'd led. "That sounds intriguing," she said. "Tell us more."

Shirley leaned against the counter, cradling her mug with both hands. "Israel was what they called a river pilot. A navigator. He helped transport rice crops and provisions up and down the waterways around Charleston. Because of those skills, Harriet Tubman hired him to help prepare for a big Union raid on the Combahee River." She smiled in triumph. "A raid that freed over seven hundred enslaved people."

Evelyn marveled at the magnitude of this exploit. "I've heard of that raid," she said. "It was featured in a recent movie about Harriet Tubman."

"Uh-huh," Shirley said. "I saw that movie too. And now a local museum, the Ezekiel Snow House, is putting together an exhibit on Harriet and her band of scouts, as they were called." Her mouth turned down. "But the curator doesn't want to include Israel Gibbs."

"Why?" Anne asked. "Because he was thought to be a scoundrel?"

Shirley shrugged. "I don't know all the details about that. The curator said there isn't enough proof that Israel helped with the raid."

"Oh no," Anne said. "That's too bad."

Sensing a challenge, Evelyn's antennae went up. She loved digging into historic archives to locate elusive answers and information. "Can we find some proof?"

"I thought maybe you could look, Evelyn," Shirley said. "If you have time."

Time was something Evelyn didn't have right now, but she wasn't going to pass up such an intriguing project. And she had a feeling that James, who was a history professor, would also be interested in helping.

"I'd love to help," Evelyn said. "I'll make the time."

"How about lunchtime today?" Shirley suggested with a grin. "Abigail offered to bring takeout."

"I'm available," Evelyn said. "What a generous offer." She often brought a lunch, but today she hadn't, thinking she would grab something in the cafeteria. A meal from Abigail's Kitchen would be a real treat. Joy and Anne also agreed to the lunch date.

Shirley set her mug on the counter and pulled out her phone. "Great. I'll shoot Abigail a text and tell her we're on."

A young woman dressed in a knee-length jumper and open overcoat appeared in the shop doorway, hovering uncertainly rather than walking right in. She had long dark hair and a heart-shaped face with a charming spray of freckles across her nose.

"Come on in," Joy called. "We're just chatting and drinking coffee."

As the young woman moved forward, Evelyn noticed the swell of her belly under her dress. This must be the customer Joy had mentioned earlier.

But rather than start browsing the displays, the young woman pulled a postcard out of her coat pocket. "Do you sell these here?" She held the card out to Joy.

Joy accepted the card, which depicted the hospital's famous Angel of Mercy statue on the front. She pointed to a nearby rack holding the angel postcards, local views, and greeting cards. "We sure do. Did you want to buy more of them?"

Pressing her lips together, the young woman shook her head. "No, I was wondering if you remembered the person who bought it." Before anyone could inquire into this odd statement, she wavered on her feet, steadying herself on the nearest display stand. "I'm sorry, I'm a little—"

Shirley pulled a chair forward and helped the woman sit. "Want to get her a glass of water, Joy?"

With a jump, Joy hurried to comply.

The woman looked up at Shirley with a little laugh. "Sorry to be so much trouble."

Shirley patted her on the shoulder. "No trouble at all, sweet pea. You relax." She took the glass of water from Joy and handed it to the woman. "I'm Shirley Bashore. And you are?"

"Megan Brooks." Megan took a long drink. "Nice to meet you. Thank you for being so kind. I was hoping and praying someone would be able to help me."

"What can we do for you, Megan?" Joy asked, standing with her hands clasped together. Her tone was tender.

The young woman's big brown eyes filled with tears. "My husband is missing. And I'm here in Charleston to find him."

Chapter Two

THE LADIES EXCHANGED GLANCES OF consternation. "What do you mean, he's missing?" Evelyn asked. She racked her brain, trying to remember if she'd seen any stories about a missing man. There hadn't been any disasters either, like a hurricane or fire, where people sometimes vanished.

The tears were spilling out of Megan's eyes in earnest now, and Joy scurried around the counter to retrieve a box of tissues. "We live in Boston, but he's been working down here in Charleston for a few weeks. Several days ago he stopped checking in, and when I try his cell number, it goes right to voice mail." She took a tissue out of her pocket and blew her nose.

"Where was he working?" Anne asked. "Did you ask there?"

"That's the thing," Megan said. "I don't know where he was working. Or living."

Evelyn noticed that her friends looked as puzzled as she felt. "I'm sorry, but I don't understand. Why wouldn't you know?" She couldn't imagine James working out of town without providing those details.

A slight smile shone through the tears. "Because he works for the government." She glanced around then lowered her voice. "Undercover."

"You mean for the FBI or something?" Evelyn asked. She'd never met an FBI agent, and this situation sounded like something out of a television show.

"Exactly," Megan said. "And I can prove it." She picked up her handbag and rooted around inside it. She pulled out a wallet and extracted a business card. "See?"

Evelyn took the card. FEDERAL BUREAU OF INVESTIGATION, it said across the top, next to the agency seal. Below the header was printed HARLEY BROOKS, SPECIAL AGENT, along with the address for the Massachusetts field office.

"Harley is your husband." Evelyn passed the card to Anne, who glanced at it and passed it on to the others.

Megan nodded. "We've been married for three years. He doesn't usually work undercover, but he was asked at the last minute to fill in and take a short assignment." She patted her belly. "With the bean due in December, he told them he couldn't be gone long."

Joy picked up the postcard. "He must have bought this here, which means he was either a patient or a visitor."

The young woman's expression went grim. "I sure hope he wasn't a patient, since that would mean he was sick or injured." Then her face lightened. "But he probably would have said something about that to you. Go ahead and read the message."

"'See you next week,'" Joy read aloud. "'All my love to you and little bean, Davidson.' No, he doesn't mention being a patient."

"Davidson?" Evelyn asked. Then she got it. "Oh, Harley-Davidson." The iconic motorcycle brand.

Megan grinned, which made her look even younger. "I started calling him that when we were dating." She rooted around in her bag again and pulled out a small stuffed turtle. "The postcard was with this, in a package postmarked Charleston." She gestured toward a stand holding stuffed animals. "I see a few more over there."

"That's a loggerhead turtle," Evelyn said. "It's our state reptile." More evidence that Harley had bought the turtle here in South Carolina, if not at the hospital. Although Angel of Mercy postcards were only available at this gift shop.

Megan picked up her wallet again. "Let me show you a picture of Harley." She slid a photograph out of a sleeve but when she stood to hand it to Evelyn, she bent over with a grimace. The photo fluttered to the floor, and Evelyn quickly retrieved it. "Oof," Megan said, wrapping her arms around her middle. "That didn't feel good." Her eyes were wide with fear. "Uh-oh. Something's happening."

Shirley swung into action, quickly taking Megan's arm to steady her. "Let's get you to the emergency room." She whirled around and pointed to the lobby. "Would one of you ladies grab that stray wheelchair? We're going to need it."

"I sure hope it's a false alarm." Anne watched in concern as Shirley wheeled Megan away. "It's too early for that baby to arrive."

Evelyn hoped so too. "At least she's in the best place possible." The emergency room staff was top-notch, and worst case, if Megan was in labor, they'd send her to the birthing unit, which was in its own wing. Evelyn said a silent prayer that mother and baby would be all right.

Joy was studying the postcard, Harley's photograph, and the turtle, lined up on the counter in front of her. She tapped the photograph, a headshot of a good-looking young man with curly brown hair and hazel eyes. "Now that I think of it, I do remember him. He came in last week."

Evelyn and Anne stared at each other in delighted shock. "That's amazing," Evelyn said. "Considering all the customers that go through here."

"He was pretty memorable," Joy said. "Charming and warm, funny, even." Her cheeks flushed with pink. "I ended up telling him my whole life story, how I moved here from Texas to be near Sabrina and the girls and then took over this gift shop. But he really seemed interested."

"He sounds like a skilled investigator," Evelyn commented. "They're good at getting people to open up."

"Did he say what brought him to the hospital?" Anne gnawed at her bottom lip as she examined the photograph. "He doesn't look familiar, but that's not surprising." Although Anne's volunteer work took her all over the hospital, she only saw a fraction of the people who came through each day.

Joy stared into space, thinking. Then she nodded and smiled. "Yes, he did. He said he was with his boss, who was attending a hospital board committee meeting."

Evelyn gave a yelp of excitement. "That's great, Joy. Soon as I have a minute, I'll check out the board trustees. We'll track Harley down." Noticing curious glances from the customers wandering into the shop, she lowered her voice to a whisper. "But we'll keep all this confidential, right? Just in case he's in trouble?"

"I think we'd better," Joy said. "Until we know more about what's going on." She tucked the turtle and the postcard under the counter and reached for the photograph next. "I'll keep these here for Megan."

"Hold on a second." Evelyn whipped out her phone and snapped a picture of Harley's handsome face. "I'm going to need that for my investigation." Then she laughed. At the questioning glances from the others, she said, "I was just thinking on the way to work how nice it would be to take a break from solving mysteries. And here we are, involved in two more already. Abigail's and Megan's."

"It's a tough job," Joy said with a wink. "But someone's gotta do it." She turned to the customer approaching the counter. "Good morning. How may I help you?"

"That's our cue," Anne said. She glanced at the wall clock. "I'd better get going."

"Me too," Evelyn said, grabbing her bag.

Outside the gift shop, the pair went their separate ways. As Evelyn hurried down the hallway toward her office, her thoughts turned to Israel Gibbs. Or, more specifically, to the possibility that there might be information about him in the Vault. The stuffy, windowless room behind the records department was jam-packed with historical records, photographs, and random items. If Israel had ever been a patient at Mercy—or worked here—she'd probably find it in the Vault. It was a place to start at least, and conveniently right inside her office. As she'd learned, the smallest bit of information could unravel a whole case.

Her steps quickened as she approached the records department, eager to begin her day. But when she opened the door and entered, a disconcerting sight met her eyes. Cliff Fox, head of maintenance, and another worker stood on stepladders, removing ceiling tiles above the archives door.

"What's going on?" Evelyn asked the men as she shrugged out of her coat and hung it on a stand.

"HVAC," Cliff said. "I'm sorry to inform you, Evelyn, but we've got a leak." He pointed to a nearby mop and rolling bucket. The floor below where they were working was still damp.

Evelyn gasped. "It's not leaking in the Vault, I hope." She imagined water pouring down and ruining all those irreplaceable papers and ledgers.

"No, ma'am," the other workman said. "We checked. And it's only dripping right now. Condensation in the ductwork."

Well, that was a relief. Evelyn relaxed until Cliff's next statement popped her bubble. "It's going to take us a few days to fix this, I'm afraid. Meanwhile, you and your employees need to stay out of this area." The normally good-humored Cliff sounded as if he meant business.

Evelyn gritted her teeth in frustration. That meant the Vault was off-limits and her plan to look for records mentioning Israel Gibbs would have to wait.

"Thank you," she finally said, mustering up her manners. It was certainly a blessing that they'd found the problem before the leaks spread to the Vault. "I appreciate all you do to keep us functioning around here."

"No problem," Cliff said. He called an instruction to his coworker and, taking the hint, Evelyn hurried over to her desk.

Doing her best to ignore the mess behind her, she sat down and logged into the system. Her in-box had forty unread emails, and the red light was winking eight new messages on her phone. A typical Monday morning in the records department.

Stacia Westbrook, one of her full-time employees, breezed into the office. A recent college graduate, the young woman was energetic and outgoing. "Hey, Evelyn," she called. Then she noticed the workers and stopped short. "Uh, what's going on?"

"Morning, Stacia. They're fixing the HVAC," Evelyn explained, her fingers still clacking away on the keys. "That area is off-limits until it's done."

"Okay." Stacia plopped a floppy leather purse on her desk then hung up her coat. "No poking around in the Vault for us."

Evelyn gave a heavy sigh. "And just when I wanted to get in there." She stopped typing and swiveled her chair to face Stacia. "Did you have a good weekend?" Stacia dated a lot, and Evelyn liked to keep a motherly eye on her romantic misadventures. She was praying Stacia would meet "the one" soon and settle down happily.

Stacia pursed her lips as she poked around in her top desk drawer. "One of my friends set me up on a blind date." She found a tube of lip balm and uncapped it. "With a guy named Bryce Stevens."

"Another blind date?" Evelyn asked. Stacia hadn't had a blind date go well, ever.

"Tell me about it." Stacia rolled her eyes and then applied the balm to her lips. "Bryce is really cute. Funny too, but we had nothing in common. He took me to this place down by the waterfront near where he works. A.J.'s Roadhouse. A bunch of his friends were there so we ended up playing pool all night. They *love* pool. Bryce is even in a league that meets Thursday nights."

"That doesn't sound so bad," Evelyn said. She'd played pool back in college and had been quite good at it.

"Playing pool was all right. And the pizza was good." Stacia threw the tube of balm into her drawer and slammed it shut. "But then his ex-girlfriend showed up, and he spent the whole night talking to her. I ended up taking an Uber home."

"Ouch," Evelyn said with a wince. "Cross him off the list."

Stacia turned her computer on. "Yep. And I told my friend never to do that to me again. She's married to a real sweetheart, so I thought she had good taste."

Evelyn's cell phone vibrated from where it lay on her desk. Shirley was calling. "They sent Megan to the delivery room," she told Evelyn. "She's doing okay, but it looks like the baby is definitely on the way. She's thirty-five weeks, so he or she will be a preemie."

Evelyn's heart twisted with concern. "I'll be praying," she said. "Let's go visit her and the baby later, once we're allowed." Fortunately Mercy's Arabella Cameron Center for Life had NICU facilities, so mother and child wouldn't have to be sent to another hospital.

"Megan said she hopes we will," Shirley said. "Oh, and don't forget. Abigail is meeting us at noon in the cafeteria. I'll try to make it, but you never know around here."

"I won't forget. I'm looking forward to it." Evelyn couldn't wait to learn more about Israel Gibbs. After they hung up, she hesitated and then made another call. If that gorgeous rose and hydrangea bouquet was still available, she was sending it up to Megan's room. The flowers hadn't been sold, and after Joy promised to have it delivered, Evelyn turned back to her tasks.

"Want some coffee?" Stacia asked a while later, breaking into Evelyn's thoughts. "I'm making a run."

Evelyn glanced up at the young woman standing beside her elbow. "Is it break time already?" She bent down and reached for her handbag. "Sure. I'd love a cup." She opened her wallet and handed Stacia some money.

After Stacia left the office, Evelyn stood and stretched. The workers were gone now, but they'd left the stepladders, caution tape draped around them. Evelyn went over to the area, not too close, and peered up at the ceiling. All that plumbing up there was a mystery to her. She stared at the Vault door with longing, wishing she could go inside. Although the contents were far from organized, they were arranged by time period. To find Israel, she'd be looking at the mid-to-late 1800s.

She couldn't do that yet, but she could search for information about Harley. Figure out where he'd worked, and for whom. The name he was using while undercover. Seated back at her computer, Evelyn brought up Harley's picture on her phone for comparison purposes before pulling up the hospital's website.

As she expected, she found a list of board trustees and their affiliations in the About Us section. A few, according to their biographies, were older and retired, so she disregarded them as possibilities. They didn't have employees. Several more were doctors affiliated with the hospital, so she disregarded them as well. Evelyn couldn't imagine Harley had been working undercover in a medical practice, since that was pretty specialized. With these trustees eliminated, Evelyn was left with several businesses to check out.

She struck pay dirt on Charleston City Trust's website, which displayed headshots of top employees, including bank president Buford Martin, hospital trustee.

Bingo. Harley worked at the downtown branch as a money manager named David Smith, and he had a direct line. Did she dare? With a shaking hand, Evelyn picked up her phone and dialed. What if he answered? That would solve the mystery of where he was—right here in downtown Charleston.

Evelyn bit her lip. But why hadn't he called his wife, then? What a thing to do to a pregnant woman. Especially one who was giving birth right now.

The phone rang. And rang. Finally voice mail kicked in. "You've reached the office of Dave Smith—"

Hi, this is Evelyn Perry, from Mercy Hospital. Your wife is in Charleston and just went into labor. No. He was working undercover. What if someone else retrieved the message? His cover would be blown.

"If you're getting this message—"

Hi, Dave. My name is Evelyn Perry. Please call me immediately about something important. Ugh. No.

"Please leave your name, number, and a short—"

Evelyn hung up, disappointed that she hadn't been able to talk to Harley. But at least she had discovered where he worked. She'd give Megan the information and let her take it from here.

Chapter Three

AT EXACTLY NOON, EVELYN WENT over to the hospital cafeteria to meet the ladies and Abigail Gibbs Johnson for lunch.

Joy waved from the corner, where she was sitting at a table with Anne and Shirley. A woman with long braids constrained by a bright scarf stood next to the table, unpacking food boxes from paper bags. That must be Abigail. Evelyn remembered seeing her when she'd visited Abigail's Kitchen.

Evelyn pulled out a chair to sit. To Abigail, she said, "I'm Evelyn. I work in the records department."

Abigail smiled. "Hey, Evelyn. Nice to meet you. I'm Abigail. I understand you're our research whiz." Her chuckle was deep and rich.

"I try," Evelyn said as she sat down beside Anne, pleased by the compliment. "I'm excited to learn more about your ancestor." Delicious aromas drifted from the containers, and she was conscious of envious looks from other diners nearby. While the hospital cafeteria offered good meals, it couldn't compete with fresh-cooked Southern soul food. "My, that smells fantastic."

"Thank you, ma'am. We do our best." Abigail opened containers and set them in the middle of the table while Shirley passed around paper plates, napkins, and utensils. Bottles of water and iced tea sat ready to drink. "I brought a variety, thought you could help yourselves."

"Oh, yum," Anne said. "I want fried chicken, mac and cheese, and green beans." She uncapped a bottle of sweet tea.

"And I'll be gobbling up that cornmeal-breaded catfish," Shirley said. "I *love* catfish."

"Fresh caught today," Abigail said. "We make everything from scratch."

Evelyn took a plump piece of chicken, a small piece of catfish, and spoonfuls of several sides—lima beans, turnip greens, and coleslaw.

Once everyone's plates were full, Anne said, "Let's say grace." The women held hands as Anne led them in a short but fervent prayer. Then they dug in with murmurs of appreciation. Evelyn went for the chicken first, enjoying the contrast between tender, juicy meat and crisp, well-seasoned crust.

"Mmm," Shirley said, wiping her mouth with a napkin. "This sure is good." The others murmured in agreement.

"Shirley said your ancestor founded Abigail's Kitchen before the Civil War?" Evelyn pulled the small notebook and a pen out of her bag, planning to take notes.

"That's right," Abigail said. "Back in 1860, which means we've been in business over one hundred and sixty years. My great-great-great-grandmother had a lodging house first. She cooked for her lodgers, and word spread how good her food was. So she opened a small restaurant." Abigail took a sip of water. "I still use her recipes."

"Why mess with perfection?" Joy asked with a laugh. "I miss my barbecue, but these ribs are definitely as good."

At Abigail's look of curiosity, Anne jerked a thumb at Joy. "Transplanted Texan." Evelyn and Shirley laughed, as did Joy, who blushed a little. Like many Texans, Joy had great pride in her state, where everything was bigger and better, they claimed. The women often teased her about it, which she took with good grace.

The restaurateur's brows went up and she smiled. "I get it." She cleared her throat. "Back to the first Abigail. Her husband was Israel Gibbs, a freeman who worked on the waterways along the coast." Her expression became uncertain. "I can't believe Cora Beth doesn't want to include him. I have a document written by his daughter, Sabra, that proves he went on the raid. And not only that, he helped Harriet Tubman scout the area."

"Cora Beth Bryant is the curator at the Ezekiel Snow House," Shirley explained before they could ask. "The one I told you about. We were really excited when she came up with the exhibit idea. Everyone knows about Harriet Tubman, but her scouts were unsung heroes. They deserve recognition too."

"The exhibit does sound wonderful," Anne said. "And I can't wait to see it. Did she give you a reason for not including Israel?"

Abigail pressed her lips together. "Only that I didn't have enough proof. She said that the events in Sabra's account need to be verified." A furrow appeared between her brows. "Over seven hundred souls were freed that night. Israel knew many of them because he ferried plantation rice crops down the river to Charleston on the boat he operated. According to Sabra, he helped spread the word that freedom was coming in advance. That way they were all ready when the Union ships showed up."

"I want to learn more about that raid," Evelyn said, imagining the boats arriving to carry people to freedom. What a joyous day that must have been.

"Me too," Joy said. "What I've read about Harriet Tubman focuses on the Underground Railroad. I never heard about the raid until recently."

"A lot more attention is being put on it now," Abigail said. "Did you know that a regiment of volunteer Black Union troops accompanied Harriet and her scouts? Most of them were enslaved refugees. They're heroes too and will be featured in the exhibit."

"As they should be," Shirley said. "And we'll get Israel included too, right, Evelyn?"

All eyes turned to Evelyn. "Yes, we will," she said, squaring her shoulders. "I'm going to get right on it." But a note of warning chimed in her mind. Was she overpromising? She had that tendency sometimes when she came across a wrong that needed to be righted. Her stomach hollowed with trepidation as she considered the possibility she might not find additional proof—or proof that Cora Beth would accept.

With an effort, Evelyn pushed away her doubts. It was too late now. She was committed 100 percent, and she would do her best, as usual. *First things first,* she reminded herself. "Can I read Sabra's account?" she asked. "Then I'll go from there."

"Of course," Abigail said. "I brought a photocopy for y'all." She put her hands together in supplication. "And I'm hoping you can go to the museum with me tonight. I'm meeting Cora Beth to talk to her about what she needs from me. From us."

"I think I can, but let me check." Evelyn pulled out her phone and brought up her calendar. She didn't have anything scheduled. "I'm free. What time?" When Abigail suggested seven, Evelyn added the meeting to her calendar.

"Thank you so, so much," Abigail said, her voice tinged with relief. She pointed at the other women. "Strength in numbers if anyone else wants to tag along."

Joy and Shirley regretfully declined, but Anne said she wanted to go. "I'll pick you up, Evelyn," she said. Anne lived about half an hour from downtown, so she'd have to drive in anyway.

"Sounds like a plan," Evelyn said. She'd also talk to James over dinner tonight and see what he suggested for historical sources.

Shirley's phone chimed and she picked it up to look at the screen. "Good news, ladies," she said, beaming. "Logan John Brooks has arrived. He's in the neonatal unit but doing well. And so is Mom."

Chills ran down Evelyn's spine at this happy announcement. "Hurray," she said, clapping. "Answered prayers." Joy and Anne also applauded, chiming in with exclamations of joy.

At Abigail's puzzled look, Shirley said, "A friend of ours just delivered a beautiful baby boy, right here in this hospital."

"That's wonderful," Abigail said. "Blessings to mother and child." She flipped open another box. "In celebration, do y'all want to try my banana pudding?"

Anne threw the others a look. "I'm so full I'm about to pop...but how can I say no?"

"I can't," Joy admitted. "Banana pudding is my favorite."

Abigail left shortly after, followed by thanks from the women for the delicious lunch. Evelyn checked the time. "I still have a few minutes, if you do," she told the others. "I wanted to give you an update on Megan's husband."

"Already?" Joy's eyes widened as she scooped up the last of her pudding. "Aren't you a wonder?"

Evelyn shrugged, hiding her pleasure at Joy's remark. "Not really. You were the one who gave me the first clue."

Anne's mouth was an O. "You mean he *does* work for a hospital trustee?" She glanced around as if afraid someone had overheard. But the adjacent tables were now empty, and everyone else in the cafeteria was minding their own business.

Evelyn lowered her voice anyway. "He sure does. I found his picture online. His name is David Smith, and he works at Charleston City Trust as a money manager." She hesitated, not wanting to admit her lack of bravery. "I called him but didn't leave a message."

"Good thinking," Shirley said. She traced her hand through the air as she swayed back and forth. "We need to get the lay of the land first." Everyone laughed at her dramatics.

"I bank at Charleston City Trust," Anne said. "We could stop by his branch and talk to him."

That was the next logical step, but Evelyn suppressed her excitement and said, "Let's talk to Megan first. She probably wants to take things from here." She sat up a little straighter, proud that they'd done the impossible and found the missing man. Well, located his place of employment, at least. Since his voice mail was active, it appeared that he was still at the bank. Although that begged the question why he'd been out of touch with Megan, to the point that she came looking for him.

Joy seemed to pick up on Evelyn's thoughts. "I wonder why he hasn't called his wife lately," she said. "I don't like the sound of that."

Anne's expression was troubled. "Neither do I. I sure hope something hasn't happened to him. Or that he hasn't abandoned his family."

"Me too." Evelyn's heart twisted in anguish. What if precious newborn Logan had lost his father—before even meeting him?

"Let's pray." Anne extended her hands, and once everyone was ready, she led them in a heartfelt prayer for the little family's well-being and safety.

Shirley's eyes were gleaming with emotion when she raised her head. "A big amen to that." She pushed back her chair. "And now I'd better scoot. Meet you in the birthing center later, during visiting hours?"

"Sounds good to me," Joy said. "I'm staying late today to do some inventory."

"I'll be there," Evelyn said. "I can't wait to see the baby." And dig further into the mystery of where his father had gone.

"Cute as a bug in a rug," Anne said, her tone adoring. "So precious." The four friends were crowded together outside Logan's unit, peeking in at the baby lying in an incubator.

Evelyn's heart swelled as she watched the little boy wave his arms and legs. "I always forget how small babies are."

"He's a good size for thirty-five weeks," Shirley said. "About five pounds, my friend said." Due to her floating assignments, Shirley had friends all over the hospital and in every department.

"When do you think he'll be able to go home?" Joy asked. "It must be so hard to have your baby stay in the hospital. I remember when Sabrina had her tonsils out. I slept in a chair all night beside her bed. And she was eleven."

"Hopefully they'll release him in two or three weeks," Megan said. "Depending on how he does." They looked up to see the new mother shuffling down the hall, dressed in a floral hospital gown and socks. Her face lit up with a huge grin. "Thanks for coming to see us. You're our first visitors."

Evelyn studied the young woman's profile as she stared in at her son, love shining in her eyes. How poignant this situation was, mother and child all alone, in a city far from home. She swallowed the lump in her throat. "Do you have parents? Or in-laws?" She held her breath waiting for the answer.

"Parents," Megan said, her eyes still on little Logan. "They live in Boston. Harley's parents both passed away several years ago."

"Will they be down soon?" Joy asked, her expression anxious.

"I wish," Megan said, her expression tightening. "My mom is having treatment for breast cancer. She can't travel right now." Then her brow relaxed. "But I sent tons of pictures already. They're over the moon with excitement."

"How about this?" warmhearted Joy said. "We'll be your surrogate moms, all four of us, until you can go home."

Tears flooded Megan's eyes. "Really? I…I can't believe…" Her voice trailed off as she wiped her wet cheeks.

Anne handed her a clean tissue. "We're Southern ladies. And we're like that. So get used to it."

Megan laughed. After dabbing her eyes and blowing her nose, she hugged each lady in turn. "I'm so glad Harley sent that postcard. If he hadn't, I wouldn't have met you."

"God sure works in mysterious ways," Shirley said. "I've given up on trying to figure Him out."

An aide came down the hall, pushing a double-decker cart holding meal trays. "Are you ready for something to eat, Mrs. Brooks? I've got your meal here."

"Great. I'm starving." Megan glanced around the circle. "I'd love it if you hang out with me while I eat."

"I've got time," Evelyn said. She was done with work for the day, plus she wanted to update Megan about David Smith. After the new mother got some nourishment into her body.

Shirley had to leave, but the other three accompanied Megan to her room in the birthing center, part of a new initiative at Mercy Hospital. The director, after seeing the success of similar programs in other states and Canada, had added family rooms where parents could spend the night while their infant was in the hospital.

"Once Logan is out of the incubator, hopefully in a couple of days, we'll be together in here." Megan climbed into bed, her meal waiting on a table tray. Joy helped push the tray into place.

"Family rooms are a wonderful addition to the maternity unit," Anne said. "Before we built them, parents of preemies had to leave at night if there wasn't room upstairs in the Mercy House. I imagine that was so hard."

"I would have hated leaving Logan." Megan pulled the lid off the plate, revealing baked chicken, potatoes, and broccoli. "Thank goodness. It's not easy being so far from home."

"Everything worked out then," Joy said. She pulled the toy turtle out of her purse. "I brought this little guy up here for Logan."

"Aw, thank you," Megan said, watching as Joy set the toy on the bedside table, along with the postcard and small photograph of Megan's husband. "I wish his dad was here to give it to him." She put down her fork and covered her face with both hands. "Here I go again." Her shoulders heaved with sobs.

Anne edged closer to the bed. She patted Megan on the shoulder and handed her a tissue. "It's all right, sugar. Let it out."

"Most of us are a mess after we give birth," Joy said. "All those hormones."

Megan laughed through her tears. "Probably that's it. But…but Harley…" Her mouth twisted with emotion.

Once the young mother had calmed down and was eating again, Evelyn moved closer to the bed. "We have news, Megan. We've figured out a couple of things about your husband."

Megan stared up at Evelyn. After swallowing a mouthful, she said, "Already? Wow, that was fast. You ladies are amazing."

Joy sent Evelyn a glance then said, "I recognized him from the photo you gave us. Last week, he came into the gift shop after attending a meeting here at the hospital. His boss is one of our trustees."

Evelyn took up the baton. "He's using the name David Smith and he's employed at a local bank called Charleston City Trust. I called his direct line, but he didn't answer. I didn't leave a message, since I wasn't sure what to say." She fished around in her handbag. "But I have the number for you, if you want to call." She set the piece of paper on the bedside table.

The young mother seemed to be absorbing this news as she ate a few more bites. After she sipped her water, she said, "Good work, but I doubt he's still at the bank. Before I flew down here, I called his boss at the FBI and told him Harley hadn't been in touch. The first time we spoke, Carson told me to hang tight, Harley had said matters were coming to a head. The next day when I called back, since Carson didn't call me like he promised, he said they were 'investigating.'"

Now the women were the ones taking in new information. "But what does that mean?" Evelyn asked. "Investigating?"

"I wish I knew," Megan said. "My mind goes round and round wondering what happened, why he dropped out of sight. Why he's not letting me know where he is or what he's doing." Her chin went up. "But I can tell you this, I trust Harley implicitly. I've never met a man with more integrity."

Evelyn believed her. That might mean that Harley hadn't disappeared of his own volition. Megan's next words confirmed her fears for his safety.

"I'm going to keep looking for my husband. And because of my circumstances"—she gestured around the room—"it'd be awesome if you helped me. If you want to, that is. But we need to be careful, really careful. Like Harley always tells me, if his cover is blown, he could die."

Chapter Four

Evelyn and her friends were stunned into silence. Megan's matter-of-fact assessment of the risk to her husband's life was chilling. Perhaps such acceptance came with the territory when your loved one worked in law enforcement.

"I'll do what I can to help you," Evelyn said at last, despite the uneasiness that came with stepping off a beaten path into possible quicksand. "But what about going to the local police?" Evelyn had met several officers while solving other Mercy Hospital mysteries, and they were excellent.

Megan shook her head. "Not yet. If I file a missing person's report, they'll send out his picture with the bulletin. It might even be featured on the news." She put a hand to her midsection. "Can't you see the headlines? 'Mom of Preemie Seeks Missing Dad.' If we do that, then his cover will definitely be blown. Not only will the criminals know David Smith's real identity, but all the work Harley's done to put them away could be compromised." Her eyes were haunted. "Plus it might put Logan in danger. I can't take that chance."

Evelyn's heart froze at the thought. "No, you absolutely can't." Megan would probably be in danger too, but how like a mother to think only of her child.

"There is something we can do that should be okay," Anne said. "Like I told the ladies earlier, I bank at Charleston City Trust. We can go over there and discreetly poke around. Find out if anyone knows anything about David Smith and his whereabouts."

A relieved expression spread over Megan's features. "Thank you so much. Normally I wouldn't be doing this, I promise you. He's been away on missions before, and I've waited at home without worrying too much. But he's never stopped communicating with me, ever. And now I have a newborn son to think about. I won't do anything to jeopardize the FBI's case, but I can't just sit here." She frowned as her voice dropped to a whisper. "I'm worried to death. Something's not right about the situation."

Evelyn had to agree. The fact that Harley was out of touch with his wife and his agency was alarming. There was a real possibility that something had happened to him. Or could it be that he was a turncoat, now working *with* the criminals?

Oh, how she hoped she was wrong on both counts. She couldn't blame Megan for investigating on her own. What would she do in a similar situation, if James suddenly vanished? Would she trust the authorities to handle it or would she try to find him herself?

Evelyn knew herself well enough to know the answer to that one.

Before leaving the birthing center, the ladies provided Megan with their cell phone numbers and extracted promises from her that she would call if she needed anything, no matter how small.

Evelyn took a last peek at lovely little Logan on her way out. *We'll find your daddy*, she told him silently, after saying a quick prayer for him. Then she started for home, glad, once again, that it was only a brief walk to Short Street, where she lived. Evelyn had grown up in this yellow clapboard house, which was narrow but deep like many Charleston houses. She had a lifetime of fond memories here.

Pulling out her keys, Evelyn climbed a flight of eight concrete steps to the front door set on the building's left. Large twin windows with Charleston-green shutters on the right adorned the first and second floors, with louvers indicating the attic above.

All was quiet in the house except for the ticking of the grandfather clock down the hall. James was still at the college, in an afternoon meeting, Evelyn remembered. She hung up her coat and then headed for the kitchen at the other end of the house. On her way down the hall, she passed wide doorways open to the dining room and living room, where tasteful neutral walls and simple, elegant furniture were set off by polished hardwood floors.

She and James had gone through the place, updating the color scheme in a way that set off wonderful historic details like the fireplaces and woodwork. The kitchen had been the last project, and Evelyn inhaled a breath of satisfaction every time she entered the room.

James had done the renovations himself, a task that had tested their marriage and his skills. But now the room was a restful medley of white cabinets and black marble counters, with a brand-new island cooktop and double ovens on the wall. Copper-bottomed pots and pans hung from a rack overhead, and stools bellied up to the island.

Evelyn set down her bag and poured a glass of cold sweet tea from the refrigerator. She was still full from lunch, so she decided on a big green salad and grilled steak for dinner. Like many men, James loved operating the grill, so that would be his chore. She would make the salad.

After pulling fresh vegetables from the hidden fridge, Evelyn began chopping and dicing. She liked salads with lots of variety, so tonight she was including lettuce, spinach, cucumbers, tomatoes, radishes, matchstick beets, and shredded carrots. The final touches were a handful of sunflower seeds and sprinkles of goat cheese.

While she worked, she thought about Thanksgiving. Maybe it was time to mix things up a bit. Whenever she made turkey, she served it with corn bread dressing from her mother's recipe. The classic Southern dish was good, very good, and James loved it.

But what about trying something new and different this year? After Evelyn tucked the covered bowl of salad in the fridge, she opened the cupboard where she kept her cookbooks. Many of them were old and battered, with stained pages and loose bindings, handed down by relatives and friends who had passed.

Evelyn loved those cookbooks best, the ones with notes in the margins and the occasional clipping slipped between the pages. Leafing through them, choosing a recipe, was like having a conversation with an old friend.

She had the cookbooks open all around and was making a list of recipes to try when the front door opened, followed by whistling. James was home.

A moment later he appeared in the kitchen doorway, a good-looking man with brown hair threaded with gray and a well-trimmed beard, dressed in a polo shirt and slacks. "Hey, Evie," he said, swooping in for a kiss. After pulling back, his gaze swept over the books. "What are you up to?" he asked with a smile.

Evelyn tapped her pen on the counter. "I'm looking up dressing recipes. Thought I'd try something new." She gazed up at him. "Aren't you tired of corn bread dressing?"

"No, ma'am." James laughed as he walked over to the fridge to pour a glass of sweet tea. "I love your corn bread dressing."

"I like it too," Evelyn said, looking back at her list. "But I'm also bored with it, so I'm going to try out a few recipes between now and Thanksgiving. Will you be my taste tester?"

James perched on the stool next to her, glass in hand. "I don't know," he said with mock dismay on his face. "That's a really big responsibility, deciding which dressing we should have."

Evelyn elbowed him. "Cut it out. But if it puts your mind at ease, I'll make the final decision. You just have to try what I come up with." She would make a couple of recipes per week, she'd decided. Small batches, to sample.

"I can do that." James swirled his glass, making the ice cubes clink, before taking another drink. "How was your day?"

Evelyn chuckled. Where should she begin? "A lot happened. But let's talk about it at dinner."

"All right," he said. "Leave me in suspense that way. What are we having?"

"Steak and salad." Evelyn turned the pages in her grandmother's cookbook. "Made the salad already, thought you could grill. It's a really nice night."

James slid from the stool. "I'd be happy to. I'll even make my famous marinade." His savory blend included Worcestershire sauce, spices, and mustard.

Evelyn made a shopping list while James moved about preparing the marinade and applying it to the steak. "I'll start the grill at five thirty," he said as he put the steak into the refrigerator. "Right now I'm heading upstairs to do a little more work." James had an office on the second floor.

"Sounds good," Evelyn replied. "I have a meeting at seven."

He paused in the doorway. "Really? Where?"

"At the Ezekiel Snow House." She smiled, teasing. "I'll explain over dinner."

Evelyn put away the cookbooks then set the table outside on the back patio, where they enjoyed eating on warm evenings. James came down and lit the grill, and soon the mouth-watering aroma of grilling meat drifted through the air.

After saying grace, the couple filled their plates and began to eat. "Okay," James said. "You've tortured me enough. What's going on?"

"Two mysteries, actually," Evelyn said, thankful for her husband's listening ear and wisdom. "One is happening right now, and the other is related to the Civil War."

As she expected, his ears perked up at the mention of the war. "Anything to do with the Harriet Tubman exhibit?"

Evelyn put down her fork. "How did you know that?"

James smiled as he cut a piece of juicy steak. "Your mention of the Ezekiel Snow House. I heard about the exhibition through the grapevine. Some of my students are writing papers on Harriet Tubman, and I've suggested they attend once it opens."

"She's a great topic. And so is the raid." While they continued to eat, Evelyn told him about Abigail Gibbs Johnson and her quest to have her ancestor's heroism recognized. "I offered to help," she concluded. "So I'm going to need your advice about where to look for more information."

"I'd love to help," James said. "And I'm eager to read Sabra's account. Abigail gave you a copy?"

Evelyn nodded. The manila envelope holding the document was in the house, waiting. "I'm hoping it'll provide clues for me to follow. Tonight I'm going to ask Cora Beth at the museum what she needs from us to prove Israel participated in the raid."

"I can understand her hesitation," James said.

"You can?" Evelyn was stung. "Why would Sabra lie about such a thing?"

James put up a hand. "I'm not saying she was lying. But good scholarship requires multiple sources. If Israel was there—and he probably was—you should be able to find evidence of that."

"I hope so," Evelyn said. "It was almost a hundred and sixty years ago." She knew James was right—after all, he taught his students proper research techniques—but she felt deflated anyway. What if she couldn't prove Israel was at the raid?

"Don't give up yet," James said. He knew her so well. "You're only getting started. Fortunately there are a lot of sources to explore. Ask Cora Beth about plantation records. If Israel Gibbs was hired to pilot boats up and down the Combahee, there will be a record of payments to him. Along with the crops he was ferrying."

"Plantation records," Evelyn repeated. She opened her small notebook, which she had brought to the table, and jotted that down.

James explained the wealth of information included in those records, many of which had been preserved and even digitized. "Once we find out who Israel worked for, we can see what's available. The historical society has some local records on microfilm."

"Why don't we read Sabra's account when I get home?" Evelyn suggested. "I'm eager to get going."

Her husband's eyes lit up. "I see the research bug has bit. And yes, I'd love to read it with you." He ate another bite of salad. "On to another topic. What's the present-day mystery?"

"It's a doozy," Evelyn said. She lowered her voice, although they were alone in the backyard and no neighbors overlooked this area. "A young pregnant woman from Boston arrived at the hospital today. She's looking for her missing husband, who works for the government."

James raised his brows. "That sounds like a premise for a thriller."

"I know, right?" Evelyn helped herself to a little more salad. "Wait until you hear what's happened so far." She went through the events of the day, including Logan's birth and her discovery of Harley Brooks's undercover identity.

Her husband regarded her with admiration. "Evelyn Perry. You're amazing."

Evelyn warmed under her husband's praise. "It wasn't that hard. I had his picture, plus Joy remembered that he worked for a trustee." She shrugged. "I put two and two together."

James's expression was grave. "Be careful, okay? If he's dropped out of sight, it's probably not for...benign reasons, shall I say. Something like this is better handled by law enforcement."

"You're right," Evelyn said, her heart aching with sorrow for the young wife's dilemma. "But Megan can't go to the police. She's worried that if she reports him missing, his cover will be blown. And if it is, he might get killed."

"Good point," James said after a moment. "But what about the FBI? Aren't they trying to find him?"

"You would think so," Evelyn said. "But they're leaving Megan out of the loop. I don't know all the details, but she was worried enough to fly down here and look for him. She said he's never, ever been out of touch this long. Even when she wasn't pregnant and close to giving birth."

James put a hand to his forehead and closed his eyes. "I don't like the sound of that. At all." His reaction confirmed Evelyn's worst fears.

"Me neither." Her voice was a croak. "What if he's already *dead*?"

Chapter Five

Evelyn's dire words seemed to echo in the quiet backyard. Instinctively she reached for her husband's hand, which was larger than hers, warm and comforting.

"I sure hope not." James squeezed her fingers. "Do what you can for her, Evie. But I want to know everything that's going on, all right? Hopefully the FBI will show up soon and take it off her shoulders. Maybe he's gone dark for a good reason."

"Let's hope." Evelyn's midsection uncoiled at James's comforting touch. "The only thing we're planning to do is go to the bank where he worked. Anne has accounts there. That's all."

"That sounds harmless enough," James said. He gave her hand a final squeeze and released her fingers. "Just be careful. And hopefully he'll show up soon."

After they cleaned up, James enjoyed a dish of ice cream, and Evelyn got ready to go to the meeting at the museum. She was waiting on the front steps when Anne pulled up in front of the house. With a wave, Evelyn ran down to the car and climbed into the passenger seat.

"Hey, Evelyn," Anne said. "How are you?"

Evelyn fastened her seat belt. "Excited. James gave me some good ideas to get started. And we're going to read Sabra's account together after I get home."

"I can't wait to hear what it says." Anne set off along the street, driving slowly. "I told Ralph about us going to the bank tomorrow. He warned me to be careful."

Evelyn laughed. "So did James." She sat back, observing the beautiful houses they passed. Their destination on Tradd Street wasn't far, only a few blocks. "I'm glad he's okay with it. It's not as if we're going to interfere with a government investigation."

"No, we're not." Anne's tone was assured. "I go to that branch a couple of times a month already. Tomorrow I'm going to open up a little savings account for Addie." Seven-year-old Adelaide "Addie" May was living with Anne and Ralph while her mother, their daughter, was on deployment. "She's been doing little chores for us and saving her money. I want to teach her about bank accounts."

"Wonderful," Evelyn said. "What's she been up to?"

"A lot," Anne said with a chuckle. She shared anecdotes about her granddaughter, now in second grade, the rest of the way.

"There's a parking spot," Evelyn said, pointing to an empty space up ahead.

After Anne parked, they gathered their bags and walked down the sidewalk to the Ezekiel Snow House, one of the oldest homes in Charleston.

"Built in 1718," Evelyn mused as they reached the pink front door. "Three hundred years old." White clapboard with black shutters, the three-story house with double-decker porches was placed perpendicular to the street, extending back into a small walled lot. As in many Georgian buildings, the third-story windows were much smaller, a style Evelyn found charming.

The front gate was unlocked, so they walked right in, entering the porch. They continued through another door into the entrance hall, a magnificent space with a curved staircase leading to the upper stories. Gilt-framed paintings hung on the deep yellow walls, and the chairs and armoire placed along the walls were obviously antiques. A chandelier tinkled gently overhead.

Voices drifted through an open doorway, so they went in that direction. This was the former parlor, featuring an ornate fireplace, pale green walls, and a selection of antique furniture. A young woman with a brown bob was standing on a stepladder hanging a picture while Abigail watched. One whole wall had been cleared for the exhibit, which consisted of several glass cases, a mannequin wearing a soldier's uniform, and wall displays.

"Hey, ladies." Abigail turned to greet them with a smile. "I'm so glad you were able to come." She led them to the young woman, who was watching them, her expression stoic. "Cora Beth, these are my friends Evelyn Perry and Anne Mabry. They're helping me find proof regarding Israel's involvement in the raid."

Finished hanging the picture, which Evelyn saw was a portrait of Harriet Tubman, Cora Beth backed down the ladder. "Nice to meet you," she said, shaking their hands. Her grip was limp and decidedly unenthusiastic, but Evelyn gave her a hearty shake and a smile anyway.

The entrance door opened and shut, and they all turned to see who had arrived. Heels tapped along the polished wood and two women appeared in the doorway. The one with blond hair appeared to be in her sixties, while the other woman, shorter and plump with fluffy white hair, had to be in her seventies.

Cora Beth charged toward the new arrivals. "Mary Lou. Lavinia. I wasn't expecting to see you tonight."

The older woman's blue eyes twinkled. "Well, I live right next door. And Mary Lou and I are so excited to see your progress."

Her identity clicked in for Evelyn. She'd heard that Lavinia Snow was a descendent of Ezekiel Snow, and that she lived next door in another gorgeous historic family home. The Snows were well known in Charleston for their philanthropy and wealth. Lavinia's tailored suit, sleek leather shoes, and designer handbag reflected her standing, as did the diamonds on her gnarled fingers and in her ears. An elegant outfit, except for the truly ugly handbag. Not only was it pea green, to Evelyn's sharp eyes it looked as though the decorative emblems were coming loose. Evelyn wondered if the hideous color meant it cost more. She wouldn't be surprised.

The other woman was gazing around with gimlet eyes in a gaunt face. Her overly slender figure was also clad in designer garb, and expensive perfume hung around her in a cloud. "You've hardly made any progress since the last time I was in," she snapped. "Think it will be ready in time?"

"Oh yes, Mary Lou, it will, I promise you," Cora said, anxiety in her tone. She fluttered back to the exhibit, pointing at the wall. "I only have a few more pictures to mount. And I'm waiting on the exhibit guide to be printed."

Mary Lou huffed. "Lavinia and I will wait in your office for your report." She turned and stormed out of the room, followed more sedately by Lavinia.

"You won't print the guide before you add Israel Gibbs, I hope," Abigail said. "You still have three weeks, don't you? That should be plenty of time to get the *updated* guide put together."

"Israel Gibbs?" A crease appeared between Mary Lou's plucked and powdered brows. "Who is that?"

Abigail whirled to face her. "He's my ancestor. He was a river pilot and one of Harriet Tubman's scouts. Although I have written proof, Cora Beth wants me to obtain more evidence. That's why I'm here, to find out what she needs."

Cora Beth's round cheeks flushed. "I'm just trying to maintain the integrity of our work here, that's all. It isn't personal, Abigail."

"So what proof do you need, besides the words of his daughter, dictated by Israel on his deathbed?" Abigail's voice rose in disbelief.

Cora Beth folded her arms. "Another eyewitness account besides his daughter's would be good," she said in a terse tone. "And what about official military records proving he was there? He must have gotten paid, right?"

Abigail made a growl of frustration in response, and seeing that tempers were rising on both sides, Evelyn cut in. "My husband is a history professor and he totally understands your point, Cora Beth." At those words, Cora Beth unfolded her arms. "He's going to help me do some research. He suggested starting with plantation records. Specifically the plantations on the Combahee River."

Cora Beth's eyes darted around the room. "I might have time to help you locate those. If they exist, that is. Call me tomorrow, okay? Right now I have to..." She waved a hand at the exhibit.

"I'll call you first thing," Evelyn said. "I'm eager to get going on this."

The curator nodded. "The deadline is two weeks from today, okay? I'll need time to write something up for the guide and then get it printed."

Two weeks. Could Evelyn do it? She'd have to. "I'll have everything for you by then, I promise." If there was information to be found.

Abigail looked at Anne and Evelyn. "I guess that's it, then. Thanks, Cora Beth."

Outside, Anne said, "Oh my, Mary Lou Martin. I wasn't expecting to see her here tonight. But she's involved in so many charities, I suppose I shouldn't be surprised."

Martin. That last name rang a bell. "Is she related to Buford Martin, president of Charleston City Trust?" Evelyn asked.

Anne pressed the fob to unlock the car doors. "I'll say. She's his wife."

Evelyn glanced back at the Ezekiel Snow House. Had Mary Lou met Harley in his undercover role? Did she have any idea where he was? If only Evelyn dared ask her.

"That was fast," James said when Evelyn walked into his upstairs office, where he was seated at his desk grading papers. "I thought you'd be gone much longer."

Evelyn sat in a leather armchair with a sigh, setting the manila envelope with Sabra's testimony onto an end table. "Me too. But we were pretty much in and out." She took him through the conversation with Cora Beth. "I'm calling her tomorrow about the plantation records, to find out if she knows where I can find them." She gave a little laugh. "I have two weeks to do the research, because of the exhibit deadline."

"That should be plenty of time," James said, his tone reassuring. He neatened the stack of papers then pushed back from the desk and stood. "I'm done here for the night. I see you brought Israel's story with you. I'm dying to read it."

"Me too." Evelyn's heart beat a little faster as she unfastened the envelope and pulled out several pieces of paper. At a glance, she could tell that Abigail had photocopied what looked like a yellowed letter, smaller than the white sheet of copy paper. The handwriting was flowing but easy to read, and the ink hadn't faded too badly.

James came to sit beside her, in the other armchair. "Want me to read it to you?"

"I'd love that." Evelyn relinquished the first page to her husband, happy that he was taking such an interest in her project. She set the rest of the papers on the table. "Hold on a minute, and I'll get us a snack."

Down in the kitchen, Evelyn made mugs of hot cocoa and put several gingersnap cookies on a plate. She loved the combination of chocolate and ginger flavors. She loaded everything on a tray and carried it back upstairs.

James was already engrossed in the document. "Starting without me?" she teased, setting down the tray.

Smiling up at her, James put the paper in his lap before accepting the mug of cocoa. "Just taking a little gander, seeing if I could understand it. Some handwritten documents are difficult to read, as you know." He took a sip of hot chocolate. "Thankfully Sabra Gibbs had great penmanship."

Evelyn took a cookie and settled back in her chair then picked up her mug. "I'm ready whenever you are."

"All right. Here we go." James picked up the page, clearing his throat. "The letter is dated October 14, 1905, and the location is Mercy Hospital."

"So Israel Gibbs was a patient, sounds like." Now Evelyn was even more eager to get back into the Vault and search for anything that mentioned Israel.

James nodded and went on. "'Testimony dictated to Sabra Gibbs by Israel Gibbs regarding the events of June 1863, when the witness was honored to assist in the fight for freedom alongside our admirable General Harriet Tubman and the brave troops of the 2nd South Carolina Volunteer Infantry.'"

"Was Harriet a general?" Evelyn broke in, hoping that Harriet had been officially commissioned, although she'd never heard that detail.

James smiled ruefully. "I'm afraid not. But that was her nickname, along with Moses."

"Moses. Leading her people to freedom." Evelyn shivered. "It gives me goose bumps."

"Me too," James said. He continued to read. "'I was born at Gibbs Plantation, along the shores of the Combahee, my precious momma's only child. I was more fortunate than most, because I was apprenticed to the river pilot that helped run rice crops downriver to the harbor. And brought provisions to the plantations upon return. Seeing my skill, Benjamin Gibbs hired me out to other plantations to navigate their boats as well. Eventually I was able to save enough to purchase my momma's freedom and my own. In 1861, I married Abigail Daniels, who owned a boardinghouse, and we were blessed with a daughter, Sabra, in 1862, and a son, Micah, in 1866.

"'But despite our personal happiness, we couldn't forget about our friends and relatives still in captivity. We felt helpless, because no matter how hard we worked, we'd never have enough to free them all. Every day I cried out to God for help to come, that like the Israelites, He would set them free.

"'And then I met Harriet Tubman. She was an answer to prayer.'" James paused.

"Wow," Evelyn said, patting her heart. "This is getting me right here."

James exhaled. "Hearing people's stories really makes history come alive, doesn't it?" He sipped his cocoa. "Pass me a cookie?"

Evelyn offered him the plate. "It's about the stories for me as well. Discovering them is like going on a treasure hunt."

Her husband saluted her with his gingersnap. "Well put."

A realization struck Evelyn. "We also now know which plantation to look for in the records," she said. "The one Benjamin Gibbs owned on the Combahee."

"Very good," James said, his eyes twinkling. "My student has earned an A."

"I'll take a kiss instead," Evelyn teased.

After giving her a fond peck, he demolished the cookie in a couple of bites then went back to reading. "'Miss Harriet asked me to join her band of scouts, and our first task was to help map Low Country islands, rivers, and shoreline. Oh, we had marine charts we used to navigate, but this was a whole other thing altogether. We went into Confederate Army territory to scope out their positions, their armaments, and fortifications. Rice and cotton storehouses too, which I was especially familiar with. And on the Combahee River itself, we mapped where torpedoes were located, with the help of the men who placed them, readily given with the promise of freedom.'"

"Torpedoes?" Evelyn broke in. "You mean bombs?"

James nodded. "Exactly. The rivers and harbors were laced with them, one reason why Charleston wasn't invaded by water." He turned back to the story, reading about the rest of the run-up to the raid, which occurred on the night of June 2, 1863, under the command of Colonel Montgomery and his soldiers. In addition to freeing people, the mission was military, with the goal of destroying bridges and railroads and cutting off supplies. "'And,'" James read, "'at the sound of the whistle, my people were to gather at the river.'"

"Gather at the river," Evelyn mused, the words of an old hymn coming to mind. There were so many Biblical connotations in that sweet command.

James laughed. "Get this, Evie. The original name of the Combahee was the River Jordan, named by the Spanish explorer who discovered it in 1520. Lucas Vázquez de Ayllón."

Evelyn gave a little gasp. "That's perfect. Our God is so wonderful."

"Isn't He?" James smiled. He tapped the page. "What a wonderful eyewitness account. I can't wait to share it with my class."

"I'm sure Abigail will be glad to let you," Evelyn said, excited at the idea that Israel Gibbs might finally be recognized for his heroism.

Israel went on to describe the journey on that night so long ago, how three gunboats had sailed up the Combahee. One ran aground, but the other two kept on. "'We crept along that river,'" James read. "'Miss Harriet stood in the prow of the lead boat, like an angel from God guiding the ship past the torpedoes. My heart pounded with fear but I tasted victory so close and sweet. At points, soldiers disembarked to run the Rebels off, but we kept on, striving for our destination. The plantations.

"'The whistle blew and the people came running. It was a melee,'" James read. "'Men, women, and children crying out, chickens squawking, overseers chasing them with threats. But somehow we got them all loaded in the lifeboats then safely onboard, including many faces so dear to me and Abigail.'" He went on, reading the final paragraphs, which spoke about the aftermath of the raid.

Evelyn was still picturing the jubilant scene. "What a wonderful story. I'm more determined than ever to help Abigail. Israel's story needs to be told."

"I totally agree." James shuffled the papers together into a neat stack and slid them into their envelope. "Want to turn on the news?" He and Evelyn liked to catch up on local news and weather in the evening.

Evelyn picked up the remote and turned on the television. As the show came on, she sat back comfortably in the chair with her mug, content to be relaxing with her husband. She was such a lucky woman.

A couple of local stories came on, and then the anchorman said, "Breaking news out of Savannah this evening. Arrests are being made in what is allegedly a smuggling ring selling knockoff designer goods." Behind his head, the screen showed a panned view of a warehouse, followed by police arresting several men. Then inside the building, handbags and clothing were strewn across long tables.

"The goods came in from overseas," the anchor said, "and were brought to this warehouse. Some of them have tags and other emblems added here. All of them are packaged for sale and shipped around the country."

James leaned forward in his chair. "This is fascinating. I had no idea that knockoffs were such big business."

"I never gave it much thought," Evelyn said, although she'd seen street vendors in cities selling obviously fake designer goods. This looked like a much larger operation. She snorted. "Although that's the only way I could ever afford a Gucci bag. Not that I want one."

James frowned. "There goes that idea for your birthday," he joked. They both laughed. "I'm really not surprised, I have to say. There's a lot of smuggling along the coast. Always has been, ever since the states were founded."

A thought struck Evelyn. Had Harley come to Charleston to investigate smugglers? Maybe his role at the bank had brought him into contact with a ring like the one in Georgia. If she could learn more about the case that had brought him here, they might be able to find him.

Chapter Six

EVELYN SIGHED AS SHE ENTERED her office the next morning, seeing that the stepladders and caution tape were still in place under the leaking ceiling. In fact, more tiles had been removed, signaling that the job was more extensive than the maintenance department had first believed.

Already at her desk, Stacia looked up from her computer with a smile. "Hey, Evelyn. How are you today?" She picked up a mug and took a sip.

"I'm great, thanks." In the process of unbuttoning her coat, Evelyn nodded at the mess. "Well, except for that."

"I hear you." Stacia rolled her eyes. "The workers were in here banging away when I arrived. Thankfully they took off."

Evelyn hung her coat up, went over to her desk, and set her handbag on the floor. "I hope they finish up soon. I really need to get into the Vault."

"You mentioned that yesterday," Stacia said. "What's going on?" Then she noticed the brooch on Evelyn's lapel. "Cute pin."

"Thanks." Evelyn touched the brooch, which was shaped like a piece of pie topped with whipped cream. "Pumpkin pie. Or sweet potato, if you prefer that. They're the same color."

Stacia leaned back in her chair. "How about both?" She took another sip of coffee. "I love Thanksgiving. All that great food, celebrating with family and friends, days off from work..."

"I love it too," Evelyn said, switching on her computer. "Oh, and yes, I am on another quest. Although I'm not sure if I'll find anything in the Vault this time."

"What are you looking for?" Stacia asked. "I continue to be amazed by the great stuff you've found in those archives. Everyone else sees a bunch of dusty papers. You find treasures."

"Very true." Evelyn glanced at the door to the Vault, remembering the mysteries they'd solved with help from those forgotten records. "I'm tracking down information about a man named Israel Gibbs, who helped Harriet Tubman free enslaved people during the Civil War. His descendant, Abigail Gibbs Johnson, is the one who asked me for help. She owns Abigail's Kitchen."

"Abigail's Kitchen is the best," Stacia said. "I go there all the time. Tell me more about Israel Gibbs and Harriet Tubman."

"It's a great story," Evelyn began. Then her phone and Stacia's rang simultaneously. "We'll talk about it later, during break."

Requests for records and patient file updates kept Evelyn busy all the way up to her usual coffee break time. Stacia was on the phone with a doctor's office, so she decided to put in a call to Cora Beth, curator at the Ezekiel Snow House.

"Good morning," Evelyn said when Cora Beth answered. "This is Evelyn Perry. How are you today?"

"Oh, hi, Evelyn." Cora Beth sounded distracted. "I'm sorry. I only have a minute. What can I help you with?"

Evelyn sighed. Surely Cora Beth couldn't have already forgotten why she was calling. "Sorry to call at a bad time," she said. "This won't take long. You said you might know where to find plantation records."

"Oh yes, that's right." Footsteps echoing and a door shutting suggested that Cora Beth was on the move. "Um, let me think. Which plantations are you looking for?"

Evelyn was glad that she and James had read Sabra's account of the raid. "The ones that used to be on the Combahee River. Benjamin Gibbs was one landowner, but I haven't had time to identify the others."

Cora Beth was silent.

"Are you still there?"

"Yes, yes, I am," came the reply. "Benjamin Gibbs, you said?" Cora Beth exhaled an audible gust of air into the receiver and Evelyn's ear. "Try the Charleston Heritage Society, over on Marion Square. They have those records on microfilm."

Evelyn made a note. "Great. Thank you, Cora Beth. I'll head over and take a peek when I have a chance." After she hung up, Evelyn stared at the phone in puzzlement. Cora Beth had been distinctly unenthusiastic, as if she didn't really want to help. Then Evelyn reminded herself to be charitable. Maybe the curator was under stress or extremely busy. She could relate to that, right?

Stacia was still on the phone, so Evelyn searched for the heritage society website on her phone, looking for their hours. During the week, her choices were lunchtime or after work. Today at lunchtime, though, she and Anne were going to the bank where Harley had worked undercover. And at some point today, she hoped to run upstairs to visit Megan and darling little Logan. Yet another task on the list was swinging by the grocery store. Tonight she was making the first test recipe, sausage and apple dressing from her mother's old cookbook. It would be perfect with the pork chops she'd already planned.

Yes, she could certainly understand the problem of being too busy. Solving two mysteries while employed full-time and taking care of her husband and home? Good thing she thrived on a challenge.

At noon, Anne popped into the records office. "Ready to go?"

Evelyn grabbed her handbag. "I sure am." Her gaze fell on Stacia, who was eating soup at her desk. "I should be back by one."

The younger woman nodded between spoonfuls. "No problem. I'll hold down the fort."

Anne jingled her keys as they strode down the hallway to the exit. "The branch isn't far, on Broad Street, but I thought we'd take my car."

"Good idea," Evelyn said. "Save some time, hopefully."

A familiar figure came bustling up to them. "Hey, ladies," Shirley called. "What are you up to?"

Evelyn glanced around to make sure no one was within earshot. "We're going over to the bank to see what we can learn about *David Smith*." She stressed his name to remind Shirley who David Smith actually was.

"Oh, I get it. I was just on my way to the NICU to see Megan."

Anne glanced at Evelyn. "Think we've got time to go say hey?"

Evelyn grinned. "Sure, if we only stay a few minutes. This way we can tell her what we're up to."

"Come on, then," Shirley said. "I don't have much time myself." As they continued toward the elevators, she said, "Abigail is so grateful you went to the museum to lend support, Evelyn. She was praising you up and down earlier when we spoke on the phone."

Evelyn cringed. "I sure hope I can live up to her expectations. But at least I have one lead to follow." As they waited for the elevator then rode upstairs, she told her friends about Benjamin Gibbs's plantation records. "The society is open late tonight so maybe I can go over after work." And then run by the store and buy ingredients for dinner.

"This is so exciting," Anne said. "Keep us posted."

They went down the corridor to the Arabella Cameron Center, saying hello to the guard before he let them inside. After pausing to admire little Logan, they went to Megan's room, where she was sitting in bed eating lunch.

The new mother put down her sandwich, her face alight. "Oh, I'm so glad to see you." She laughed. "I'm getting a little lonely up here."

Evelyn could imagine. Far from home, her husband missing... anyone would struggle in this situation.

"Even with the staff constantly in and out?" Shirley asked as she tweaked the bedding into place.

Megan's face flushed. "Everyone has been wonderful. I didn't mean—"

Shirley patted her shoulder. "I know, sugar. Just teasing."

"How's the baby?" Anne asked. "I think he's getting cuter every minute."

"Isn't he?" Beaming proudly, Megan picked up her sandwich again. "He's doing really well, they said this morning." She took a nibble, chewed, and swallowed. "We're doing kangaroo care after lunch."

At Evelyn's inquiring look, Shirley explained. "Kangaroo care is another term for snuggling. Up close and personal so mother and baby can bond."

"It's especially important because I can't hold him all the time, not with his feeding tube and oxygen," Megan said, crunching a piece of celery. "And believe me, I want to."

"I know you do," Anne said. "I was practically glued to my daughter Lili when she was an infant."

Megan asked Anne a question and the two chatted about new mother things for a minute, with Shirley interjecting her wisdom. Evelyn heard a man speaking out in the hall. "I'm looking for Megan Brooks," he said. Her heart leaped. What if that was Harley? Evelyn edged back a couple of feet so she could get a better view.

But the man striding toward the room was older, with close-cropped gray hair, a square jaw, and piercing blue eyes. He wore an expensive gray wool suit, attire worn in the South mostly by government officials or bankers.

The newcomer tapped on the doorjamb with his fist. "Sorry to intrude." His eyes focused on the woman in the bed like laser beams. "How are you, Megan?"

Megan pushed herself to a more upright position. "Carson. Is there any news?" She glanced at the ladies. "Carson Lewis is my husband's boss."

From the FBI. Evelyn studied the man closely, never having met an FBI agent before. As the agent approached, Anne and Shirley moved back from the bed to give him room. He opened his mouth then frowned at the trio looking on. "Can you give us a little privacy, please?"

"They can hear whatever you want to say." Megan lifted her chin, defiance flashing in her eyes. "They're my friends. And besides you, the only people I know in Charleston."

Carson hesitated, a crease appearing between his brows. Then he gave a brisk nod. "Fair enough." He crossed the room to the bedside. "Are you doing all right?" His tone had softened, and a slight smile transformed his chiseled face. "How's the baby?"

"He's small but healthy," Megan said. "Absolutely gorgeous." She leveled a gaze at him. "Where is my husband?" She spoke through gritted teeth.

The agent lowered himself to the bedside chair. He sat leaning forward, hands clasped between his open knees. "I'm sorry to tell you this, but we don't know."

Megan drew back as though stung. "What do you mean, you don't know?" Her laugh was bitter. "Do you often misplace your agents?"

"Megan, please," Carson said, shifting in his seat. Slanting a look at Evelyn and her friends, he said, "We're working as hard as we can to locate him. At times, agents need to go into hiding, in which case he'll be in touch soon."

"Because he's in danger," Megan said. Her tone was flat, but the color in her cheeks revealed her alarm.

"Yes, ma'am. The other possibility is that he's dropped out of sight of his own volition." His eyes narrowed, never leaving her face. "If you hear from him, we want to know immediately."

His words seemed to strike Megan like a slap, her eyes widening and her mouth dropping open. "What? Are you seriously suggesting that my husband might have gone *rogue*?" Her fists clenched. "It's bad enough that he's missing." Her voice thickened. "And probably afraid for his life."

Shirley rushed forward. "Hold on, now. Don't you be upsetting a new mother that way." She sent Carson a reproachful glare.

Megan put out her hand. "I'm okay, Shirley. Honestly."

At seeing Megan's distress, Evelyn's caring heart ached. "Has he ever given you reason to doubt his loyalty?" she asked Carson. "Or his integrity?"

Seeming to draw strength and determination from Evelyn's outburst, Megan lengthened her spine. "She's right, Carson. I know my husband, and he would never betray his country." Her face began to crumple, and her voice shook. "Or me and our son." She blinked rapidly but held back the tears.

Anne put her hand on Evelyn's arm. "Why don't we give them some privacy? I'm sure they have things to discuss."

"I would appreciate it," Carson said, gratitude in his eyes. "I'm sure you ladies understand."

Evelyn allowed herself to be tugged away, her eyes fastened on Megan's forlorn face. "We'll be back later, okay? We're just stepping out for lunch." She pressed her lips together in annoyance. They hadn't even had a chance to tell Megan their plans. "And swinging by the bank." The spark flaring in Megan's eyes told Evelyn *message received*.

Shirley neatened the items on the bedside tray. "You need anything, press the call button, sweet pea, okay?"

Megan nodded.

Out in the hall, the trio huffed and exclaimed, quietly of course so as not to bother the other patients.

"My heart sure goes out to that child," Shirley said, shaking her head. "I don't know which is worse. Her husband being in danger or a criminal on the run."

"I suppose the FBI has their reasons for believing what they do," Anne said slowly. "I pray they're wrong."

Anne was always the tempered, balanced one, and Evelyn appreciated that. But right now her own feelings were torn between righteous anger and a sinking feeling in her belly. "Innocent until proven guilty," she said, more to reassure herself than the others. "That's what I'm going by."

They paused next to the nursery, where a nurse was tending Logan. She smiled up at them over her mask then looked back down at the baby. Evelyn, standing between Shirley and Anne, felt a soft, warm hand slip into hers. "Let's say a prayer," Shirley whispered. Evelyn took Anne's hand, closing her eyes as Shirley uttered a short plea for Logan and his parents.

"Thanks, Shirley," Evelyn said as they released hands. "I feel so much better." The turmoil had lifted right off her shoulders, leaving her calm and at peace.

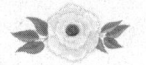

The bank was on Broad Street, one of Charleston's main thoroughfares. In fact, this avenue lined with historic buildings was a marker, with the neighborhoods "south of Broad" considered highly desirable with their views of the harbor.

Anne slid into a parking space a few buildings away from the bank. "Ready?" she asked. She grabbed her parking card for the meter from the console.

Evelyn inhaled a deep breath. "Yes. Yes, I am." Carson's news hadn't dampened her determination to locate Harley Brooks. In fact, quite the opposite. His wife and child needed him.

Charleston City Trust was housed in a building both opulent and dignified. Four massive columns guarded a shallow portico sheltering the entrance. After passing through gold-framed glass doors, they entered an echoing and spacious lobby. Potted palms dotted the black-and-white tile floor, and at the far end was the teller line behind a gleaming counter. Several desks were scattered about, and at the rear, Evelyn spotted several closed doors to offices.

"I usually go to Emily," Anne said, leading the way to a customer service representative with flowing brown locks and pretty features. Her fingers flew across her keyboard as she typed away.

"Hey, Mrs. Mabry." Emily looked up from her computer. "How can I help you today?"

Evelyn and Anne sat in the customer chairs, and while Anne chatted about setting up the new account, Evelyn looked around the room. Near the wall was an empty desk, the only one in the room. An array of vintage Charleston photographs lined the wall behind the desk, giving her the perfect excuse to wander in that direction.

She rose to her feet and then casually made her way across the bank floor. Tellers glanced her way, but they were all busy with customers. Keeping her gaze on the photographs, Evelyn gradually veered toward the empty desk.

Holding her breath, she squinted at the nameplate resting on the front edge. DAVID SMITH. *Yes.* Evelyn swallowed a shout of jubilation. *Act casual*, she told herself. As she sidled past, she covertly checked the desktop. Computer monitor, calendar blotter, box of business cards, pen stand. And a snow globe paperweight on a stand.

Pretending to adjust her shoe, Evelyn took a closer look. Inside the paperweight was a mountain that looked like a volcano. She wondered what happened when you shook the globe. Then she scanned the calendar. Although notes had been scrawled inside the boxes, they stopped the previous Wednesday.

A man cleared his throat behind her. "Can I help you?"

Chapter Seven

STILL BENT OVER HER SHOE, Evelyn whirled around and almost fell, forced to grip the side of the desk to steady herself. The man was stocky and of medium height, with a fleshy face and pale hair combed straight back from his forehead. His suit was perfectly tailored, and he wore a class ring from Duke University.

A splash of cold shock drenched Evelyn as she recognized Buford Martin, bank president and hospital trustee. What if he knew she was a hospital employee? Would he report her to the hospital administrator for snooping?

Evelyn squared her shoulders. She hadn't been doing anything wrong. "I'm here with my friend," she said, waving toward Anne. "I came over here to look at these old photographs. They're stunning."

Buford turned toward the display, which featured views of Broad Street a century in the past. "They're quite nice, aren't they? My great-great-granddaddy was president then."

No way out but through. Evelyn put out her hand. "Are you the bank president? I'm Evelyn Perry. I met your wife at the Ezekiel Snow House last night."

Buford shook her hand, his palm as meaty as the rest of him. "Buford Martin. Nice to meet you, ma'am." He chuckled. "The

Ezekiel Snow House is one of Mary Lou's little projects. She has so many, I can barely keep up."

"I'll bet," Evelyn said.

To her relief, he dropped her hand and edged away. "Have a nice day, Ms. Perry. Now if you'll please excuse me…" He waved a hand. "My work is never done, I'm afraid."

"Of course," Evelyn said. "Don't let me keep you." She watched as he went into the closest office, a brass plate announcing it belonged to the bank president. Once he was safely out of view, she slipped her phone out of her pocket and took a quick shot of the desktop. She'd show it to Megan later, see if she recognized the paperweight. It wasn't standard bank equipment like the blotter and business cards, which was odd, now that Evelyn thought about it. Her heart gave a lurch. Why would he leave anything personal behind? That spoke to a hasty exit.

Evelyn grabbed one of David Smith's business cards. Maybe Emily knew where he had gone.

Anne threw her a wide-eyed look when Evelyn rejoined her at Emily's desk. Evelyn raised her brows to let Anne know she'd fill her in later.

"All right, Mrs. Mabry," Emily said as her printer spit out pages. She slid a piece of paper across the desk. "Please sign this."

While Anne and Emily took care of paperwork, Evelyn waited, the business card in her hand. Once they were done, she gave Emily the card. "I'd like to speak to David Smith." Oh, would she. "Do you know when he'll be in?"

Emily looked over her shoulder at David's desk then turned her attention back to the card. "I'm not sure…I don't think he works here anymore." She pushed the card back to Evelyn.

"Really?" Evelyn asked. Her heart was hammering. "Did he start a job at another bank?"

The customer service representative gnawed at her bottom lip, obviously conflicted. "I don't know." She swiveled in her chair, which squeaked a little. "One morning I came in and he was gone. When I asked where he was, no one seemed to know."

Evelyn wanted to ask more, such as when he had actually vanished, but that would look strange. Not that this situation wasn't odd as well. When staff left the hospital, everyone knew why for the most part, confidential human resources information aside, and where they had gone. If they'd retired, taken a new job, or moved away, for example.

"Well, if you hear that he's working somewhere else, let Anne know," Evelyn said. "A friend highly recommended him."

"We'll probably be replacing him soon," Emily said. "And whoever we get will do a wonderful job for our customers."

Anne tucked her copy of the paperwork in her handbag. "I'm sure. I've always been happy here." She turned to Evelyn. "Ready?"

Evelyn nodded and stood. "Nice to meet you, Emily." As the young woman murmured wishes for a good day, the lobby doors opened and two familiar faces walked in.

Detective Rebekah Osborne and Officer Jason Williams, both from the Charleston Police Department.

Surprised to see the officers, Evelyn stopped dead in the middle of the lobby. Something about their intense expressions made her think they weren't here on personal business.

Anne raced ahead, waving a hand in greeting. "Hey, Detective Osborne, Officer Williams. What brings you to the bank?" With a silent laugh, Evelyn scooted to join her friend.

Officer Williams slid a glance toward his superior. "We can't discuss that, ladies." The expression on his young face was stern.

"Oh," Anne said, her voice rising. "I get it." She patted her handbag. "Evelyn and I popped over here during our lunch break so I could open an account for my granddaughter. Got to start them saving early, right?"

"Right," Rebekah said, edging past Anne and Evelyn. "Now if you'll excuse us…"

"Sure thing," Anne said, her tone still bright and cheerful. "Y'all have a good day, you hear?"

"See you at the hospital," Evelyn added as the officers walked across the lobby. During past cases, both officers had visited the hospital in the course of their investigations. She started to push open the exit door, but Anne hissed a whisper to wait.

"Don't you want to see where they go?" Anne asked. She opened her handbag and began to rummage around as if searching for something. Meanwhile the two officers strode through the bank without stopping, nodding at the curious employees they passed.

Evelyn gripped Anne's arm. "They're going to see the bank president." Indeed, after stopping to speak to a uniformed security guard, the officers knocked on Buford Martin's door. Then they walked inside and shut the door firmly behind them. "I wonder what's going on."

Anne thrust out her bottom lip. "I have the feeling it involves David Smith." She ushered Evelyn out the door, still speaking in a low voice. "He disappears and the police come to call? It's got to be connected."

Evelyn's belly churned in distress. "Maybe they're looking for him after all," she said. "We need to tell Megan."

"Yes, we do." Anne retrieved her keys from her bag. "Want to grab sandwiches to go? That'll give you more time." As a volunteer, Anne's hours were more flexible.

"Sure," Evelyn said as they walked down the sidewalk, although her mind wasn't on lunch right now. "I think Emily knows something is wrong. She was acting scared."

Anne unlocked the car. "I don't know if she was scared, exactly, but she certainly didn't want to talk about David Smith."

Evelyn slid into the passenger seat and immediately rolled down the window, since the noontime sun had turned the car into a furnace. "Definitely not, which is strange all by itself. Maybe the bank president warned them not to talk about him for some reason."

Anne started the car and then glanced in the mirrors and over her shoulder, preparing to pull out into the street. "Speaking of the bank president, what did he say to you?"

"Oh my," Evelyn said as she fastened her seat belt. "I almost had a heart attack. I was pretending to fix my shoe, but I was actually looking at David Smith's desk when Buford Martin came up behind me. He asked if he could help me, so I said I was interested in the old photographs, which I was."

Anne set off down the street. "Did you see anything interesting on David—I mean Harley's desk?"

Evelyn scrolled through her phone. "Nothing that told me where he went, unfortunately. But his calendar didn't have any notes after last Wednesday." She had a thought. "I wonder if Joy can confirm which day he came into the gift shop."

"That might be hard," Anne said. "I don't think the sales are that closely itemized."

Evelyn realized she was right. The receipts only showed the department—such as floral or gift—rather than the actual item. "I know what I can do. I'll look up the committee meeting dates. He said he was there at a meeting, remember?"

"Now that you mention it, yes," Anne said. She halted at a traffic light. "That's what I like about you, Evelyn. Well, one of the many things. You don't take no for an answer."

"In this case, I refuse to," Evelyn said stoutly. "Every time I even think about quitting, Logan's little face comes into my mind."

On the way back to the hospital, they stopped by a favorite sandwich shop, where Evelyn popped in and bought lunch to go. She still had ten minutes on her lunch hour when they arrived back at the hospital, so they raced to Megan's room.

Megan was seated in the armchair, snuggling the baby. She looked up with a beatific smile. "Hi, there. Back already?"

Evelyn had been planning to tell Megan about the police arriving at the bank, but she swallowed back that disturbing news for now. "If this isn't a good time, we can come back."

"You're fine." Megan stroked the baby's cheek with her finger. "Is there anything new?"

Anne gave Evelyn a nod, so she pulled out her phone. "I did find your husband's desk, with his nameplate." Megan glanced up sharply, and Evelyn winced. "I'm sorry, but he wasn't there. However, I did see this on the desk." She scrolled to the picture of the volcano paperweight. "Does that look familiar?"

Megan studied the paperweight then nodded. "Yes, it's his. My father gave it to him, and he loves it." She smiled. "He says he lets the volcano blow its top so he doesn't have to."

"Okay," Evelyn said, making a mental checkmark. "We know where your husband worked and that's he's not there anymore. I also peeked at his calendar, and there wasn't anything written on it after Wednesday last week."

Megan's attention was on her son, but she said, "That fits. I got the package on Friday. Priority. So he mailed it Wednesday. I never heard from him after Wednesday night." Despite her calm, matter-of-fact words, a tear trailed down her cheek and landed on the baby's blanket.

Anguish rose in Evelyn's chest, choking her. "We're going to find him, Megan," she whispered fiercely. "Have faith."

Megan looked up. "I'm trying," she said. "Honestly. Faith is the only thing I have to hang on to. That and my precious baby boy."

Anne moved closer and took Evelyn's hand. Then she said a short prayer, asking God's blessing on Megan and her family and for Harley's safe return.

"Thank you both," Megan said, sniffling. "Whenever I have doubts, I remember one thing. God led me here to you." She looked down at Logan. "Where would we be, sweet pea, without our friends?" she murmured.

Evelyn inhaled, releasing her worries and fears. She would take her next steps under God's direction and leave the outcome to Him.

"I can't believe it's time to go already," Stacia said, signing off her computer.

Evelyn noted the time with disbelief. "This afternoon really flew by, didn't it?" Thankfully she'd been able to push the two mysteries out of her mind and focus on the tasks at hand, which were many.

"What are you doing tonight? Anything fun?" Evelyn asked her young helper as she put away her work. To save time, she was taking the bus to the heritage society then returning the same way. James would be home by then, so she could take the car and go to the grocery store. Sometimes her plans required the logistics skills of a general.

"Not really. I plan to relax." Stacia's smile was rueful. "But guess who texted me."

Evelyn was able to guess very easily. "Not your blind date?"

"Uh-huh." Stacia nodded emphatically. "He wanted a second chance."

"I hope you told him no," Evelyn said, annoyed on Stacia's behalf. "What a nerve."

"No kidding." Stacia placed some files in her in-box, to be dealt with the next day. "Things must not have gone well with his ex after all." Her smile was cheeky.

Evelyn snorted. "Probably not. I think you dodged a bullet, my dear." She pushed her chair in then picked up her handbag and retrieved her coat from the peg. Not that she needed it this afternoon. The temperatures had continued to rise all day.

Once on the bus, Evelyn rode north to Marion Square. The former military parade ground encompassed over six acres of green space and was a popular spot to gather. After she got off, she made her way to the Charleston Heritage Society, which was housed in a beautiful three-story brick building trimmed with rough-cut stone and adorned with arched windows. The entrance was inset under a wide arch, an effect that made Evelyn feel as though she were entering a castle.

Inside, the ceilings were high and the atmosphere hushed. The foyer was square, with stairs on one side and archways leading to the rooms beyond. A bell sat on the reception desk, which was empty.

"Hello?" Evelyn waited for a few moments, and when no one came or responded, she pressed the bell. After another minute, she rang it again.

"Coming," a voice called from the back room, accompanied by brisk footsteps on the polished floors. A petite woman with fluffy gray hair charged through the archway. She stopped, smiled, and patted her chest. "Whew. Sorry. I was way in the back, in the storeroom. I always lose track of time in there." By her accent, Evelyn guessed she was from the Midwest.

"It sounds like we're kindred spirits," Evelyn said. "At the hospital, we have what we call the Vault. It's full of fascinating old stuff."

"I'll bet," the woman said, a light in her eye. "I'm Patricia Cooper, one of the volunteers. And you are?"

"Evelyn Perry. I'm here to look at plantation records." Evelyn dug in her handbag and pulled out her notebook and pen.

"I see you're prepared, but you'll be able to print off what you need." Patricia gestured. "Come with me." She set off across the lobby and Evelyn followed. "Those plantation records are fascinating. They provide a real window into life back then."

"That's what I've heard," Evelyn said as Patricia led her through an exhibition room. Glass cases held all kinds of memorabilia, and mannequins were dressed in nineteenth-century style, including a huge hoopskirt ball gown.

Patricia opened a door and switched on a light. "The microfilm readers are in here." The room was small, packed with shelves full of books and binders and a row of file cabinets along one wall. Two microfilm readers sat on desks.

While Evelyn set her notebook and handbag down on one of the desks, Patricia bustled to the file cabinets. "Is there a particular plantation you're interested in?" she asked, holding a drawer handle.

"I'm researching the Benjamin Gibbs plantation on the Combahee River," Evelyn said. "He grew rice there."

"The Combahee River?" Patricia mused as she leafed through the drawer contents. "I've been hearing a lot about that lately."

"The Ezekiel Snow House is doing a special exhibit on the raid led by Harriet Tubman up that river," Evelyn said. "I'm looking for information about Israel Gibbs, who was a river pilot."

"River pilot. What a fascinating occupation." Patricia paused, shaking her head. "I haven't heard of him. But that doesn't mean much since I'm a recent transplant from Ohio." She went back to her task. "But I love history, so here I am. I'm learning about this wonderful city as I go."

"I'm a lifelong resident," Evelyn said. "And I'm still learning. Every now and then a project comes along, and I have so much fun digging into it."

Patricia looked over her shoulder with a glance of complicity. "I always say it's like being a detective. Following the clues and seeing where they lead."

"Exactly." Evelyn browsed through the book titles on the closest bookshelf. One binder was labeled, ORAL HISTORIES. Those must be fascinating, firsthand accounts of life in the past.

Patricia made an exclamation as she shut the drawer. Then she opened another and began to search through the contents, muttering to herself.

"Is something wrong?" Evelyn asked.

The volunteer didn't answer for a moment as she continued to paw through boxes of microfilm. "I can't find the records for the Gibbs Plantation," she said as she shut the drawer. "That particular box is missing."

Chapter Eight

Evelyn rocked back on her heels. "What do you mean, missing? His plantation is included in a list on your website."

Patricia put up both hands. "I'm sorry, Evelyn. I can't locate it." She whirled around and grabbed a binder on top of the file cabinet. "Let me check the list." Humming to herself, she leafed through the pages. She held up the binder so Evelyn could view the alphabetical list. "It's right there, see? But I can't find the box."

"Where did it go? Was it misfiled?" Evelyn asked.

"I checked that," Patricia said. She tapped two drawers in the file cabinet. "All our microfilm is here and here."

A terrible suspicion began to take root in Evelyn's mind. "Did someone take it?" But why would someone steal microfilm? A printed copy could easily be made, if someone wanted one. It was a real puzzle.

Patricia pulled her head back. "Who would do that? Those rolls are no good without a reader."

"You're right about that," Evelyn said, studying the two machines. They weren't very common anymore with the move to digital records. She pushed aside her uncomfortable thoughts. "Okay, moving on. Do you think another society might have those records? I'm sure that wasn't the only copy." She hoped.

Patricia brightened. "I'll make some calls. I can't guarantee anything, but if the Gibbs Plantation records are to be found, I'll locate them."

"I would really appreciate that," Evelyn said. "And not to press you or anything, but I have a deadline." She thought back to what Cora Beth had said. "Thirteen days, to be exact."

"Plenty of time then," Patricia said. "I'll make the calls this afternoon or tomorrow morning. What's the best number to reach you?"

Evelyn jotted her name, phone number, and what she was looking for on a page in her notebook and then ripped it out and handed it to the volunteer. "Thank you so much, Patricia. You've been a huge help."

"No problem." Patricia waved the page. "And you better believe I'll tell the board about this situation. We can't have things go missing like this." She sighed. "We probably should put in security cameras after all. They've been talking about it."

"Good idea," Evelyn said. "Although I hate to think people would stoop so low as to steal from the heritage society."

"Me too. It's really disappointing." Patricia started to move toward the door. "Please feel free to stay and browse, but I've got to get back to work."

Evelyn glanced at the time on her phone. "Normally I'd love to, but I'd better get going." Without a clear-cut research mission in here, she would be wasting her time. She'd talk to James later and figure out her next steps. Maybe she wasn't sure what they were at the moment, but she knew one thing. She wasn't going to let this setback deter her.

"What's in this?" James prodded the dressing on his plate with a fork then looked more closely. "Is that a prune?"

"Yes," Evelyn admitted. "This is prune, apple, and sausage dressing." She scooped up a bite and tasted sweet and savory flavors bursting on her tongue. "I know it sounds strange, but it's not bad. Try it." The recipe was from her grandmother's cookbook, marked with a pencil notation stating, *Very good*.

James took a tentative bite then chewed and swallowed. "It tastes fine. As long as I don't think about the prunes."

Evelyn sighed. "Pull them out. I guess I won't make this recipe for Thanksgiving." She cut into her pork chop.

"I don't know why you have to do something different," James said as he gingerly extracted prunes with his fork. "I love your dressing. Why mess with success?"

"Good point," Evelyn said. "But I'm having fun. So please humor me."

Her husband's eyes twinkled. "Of course. I'm your willing victim—er, taste taster."

Evelyn smiled. "Don't worry. I'll victimize you again soon. I've found a few more recipes to try." Hopefully one of those would go over better than this concoction.

They ate in silence for a moment, and then James asked, "How was your day? Did you make any progress?"

"I don't know where to begin," Evelyn said. "The FBI showed up at the hospital today. Well, one agent did."

James's brows shot up. "Really? Is there news about Megan's husband?"

"Not yet," Evelyn said. She relayed the gist of the conversation with Carson Lewis. "I refuse to accept his theory that Harley might have gone rogue," she concluded. "Carson Lewis is wrong. He needs to do his job and find Harley fast."

James opened his mouth, started to speak, and then paused before saying, "I don't blame you for being protective of Megan—"

"And Logan," Evelyn broke in. "What kind of father would abandon his baby?"

His expression grew serious. "If he did, it would mean that Megan totally misjudged his character." At her quick exclamation, he put up a hand. "Hold on, I'm not saying she did. You're right, we don't know enough yet."

Evelyn was relieved that James had come around to her point of view. "Anyway," she said, "Anne and I went to the bank where he worked, during lunch." She told him about going over to David Smith's desk and seeing his cherished paperweight still in place. "From his calendar, it appears his last day at the bank was Wednesday. We also think he mailed the toy turtle and postcard to Megan that day."

"Toy turtle and postcard?" James inquired.

"Oh, didn't I tell you? The postcard he sent her was from the hospital. A picture of the Angel of Mercy. And we think the stuffed toy came from the gift shop." Evelyn's tone was triumphant. "Does that sound like a man who was planning to run off?"

"You're right," James said. "In that case, he'd be more likely to mail bundles of cash."

"Speaking of bundles of cash," Evelyn said. "Two Charleston police officers showed up as we were leaving the bank. I'm really curious what they were doing there. But of course they wouldn't say."

"Did you ask them?" James stared at his wife. "That would be pretty bold."

"No, but Anne did." Thinking back to the scene, Evelyn laughed. "We know them from the hospital. Rebekah Osborne and Jason Williams."

"What did they say?" James wiped his mouth with his napkin, and Evelyn noticed that he'd cleaned his plate. Well, except for the prune pieces lined up along the edge.

"Oh, they wouldn't tell us anything," Evelyn said. "But I'm sure we'll find out soon enough." She and her friends had an inside police department source in hospital security guard Norm Ashford, a former police officer. Hopefully they could catch up with him tomorrow.

James got up and cleared their plates. "Should I put on a pot of decaf? I have a bunch of work to do tonight, unfortunately. Grading papers."

"I'd love a cup," Evelyn said. "We have cookies or ice cream if you want dessert." Watching him move around the kitchen, she thought about her other project. "Before you start grading, can you help me with something? I ran into a total dead end today at the heritage society." When she had his full attention, she said, "The microfilm roll I need is missing. According to the volunteer, it used to be in the file, but now it's gone."

James's eyebrows shot up. "Seriously? That's a bummer."

"I know." Evelyn traced her finger along a pattern in her place mat. "The volunteer is going to contact other places for me."

"Hopefully she'll be able to find another copy." James rinsed the plates and put them into the dishwasher. "I recommend you keep going while you wait."

"Any ideas?" Before he could answer, Evelyn slid out of her seat. "Hold on. I need to take notes." She dashed out to the hall, where she had dropped her handbag, and grabbed her notebook. Then she slid back into her seat, opened the book, and gazed at James with expectation.

James laughed. "I don't think I have any students as eager as you." His expression softened. "Or as lovely."

A wave of heat flamed in Evelyn's cheeks. "Oh, you charmer." After all these years, he could still make her blush.

The coffee finished brewing, and James poured two mugs. "The plantation records are important to establish the facts about Israel's work as a river pilot. But a really good source for anyone who served in the military are pension records."

Evelyn tapped her pen. "Do you think Israel going along on the raid would have qualified him for a military pension?" She had to admit not knowing much about how the process had worked.

"I would think so." James leaned his elbows on the counter. "He also helped Harriet Tubman before the raid. I know that she applied for a pension based on her service, which spanned years."

"Did she get one?" Evelyn asked. Nowadays many women served in the military, but no doubt in Harriet's day, there were very few.

"That's a long story," James said. "The bottom line is, she had to fight for decades to get a pension, and even then she didn't get everything she was entitled to." He shook his head. "It was a very disappointing outcome." He explained how Harriet had first gotten a pension as a widow, and then later only for service as a nurse, ignoring her work as a spy.

Evelyn couldn't speak for a moment, her justice-loving heart outraged by this turn of affairs. "What a shame," she finally said. "I'm glad her heroism is finally getting recognized. And that's why I'm not giving up on Israel."

"I wouldn't," James said. "You're only getting started. Anyway, back to the pension records. Applying for pensions back then was a very intensive process. You didn't just fill out a form and send it in, not in the days before social security numbers and computerized service records. People used to collect affidavits regarding their military service. They often included medical histories in the case of disabilities. If widows applied, they had to include marriage records and birth certificates of any children. So there's often a wealth of information in those files."

"Where can I find them?" Evelyn asked. "Do you know?"

James picked up his mug. "I sure do. Why don't you bring your tablet to the study? You can search online while I work."

They went upstairs, where James guided Evelyn to certain web addresses before he sat down at his desk, where a stack of papers waited.

Evelyn poked around the sites for a while, figuring out how they worked. She realized that Israel Gibbs would not qualify for a Confederate pension, since he'd been helping the Union Army. The second thing she noticed was that very few South Carolina pension records were online, unlike in other states, such as Florida and Georgia.

That meant searching a national index—and paying for copies of records. Before she went that far, Evelyn gave Abigail a call at the restaurant. She didn't have her personal cell number yet.

A young man answered the phone. "Good evening. Abigail's Kitchen. How may I help you?" Dishes clattered in the background among a clamor of voices.

"Oh, I'm sorry," Evelyn said. "Are you in the middle of the dinner rush?"

"Just finishing up, ma'am. What can I do for you?"

Evelyn gave her name and said she'd like to speak to Abigail if she wasn't too busy. The phone clunked down, and she heard the young man shouting for Abigail. A moment later, Abigail came on the line. "Evelyn. How y'all doing? Any luck yet?"

Oh, how Evelyn hated to disappoint her new friend. "Getting there. Nothing substantive yet."

"Hold on. I'll go somewhere quieter." Footsteps sounded and a door shut, quieting the bedlam of the kitchen. "So tell me." Abigail's voice was eager. "What have you found out?"

Evelyn took a deep breath. "I'm on the trail, but I haven't located Israel's records yet. But I will." Before Abigail could say anything, she said, "A couple of things. It would be really good to get his birth date and date of death if you have it. Just in case there's more than one Israel Gibbs."

"I have his information right here." Abigail shuffled through papers then read off dates while Evelyn hastily took them down. "We can visit his grave if you want. He's in the Mother Emmanuel AME burial ground. We put a new flag out every Veterans Day, which is coming right up. You can join us if you want."

Veterans Day was next week, Evelyn recalled. "I'd like that," she said. She would bring flowers, she decided, one of Joy's beautiful bouquets. "Just to confirm, Israel lived in Charleston after the war?"

"Yes, he did," Abigail said. "He and Abigail lived in the boardinghouse the rest of their lives."

"One more thing and then I'll let you go," Evelyn said. "Some records are online and there may be a small fee to access them. Or I might need to pay a researcher to retrieve paper copies from the National Archives. Do you want me to go ahead?"

"Yes, I do," Abigail said after a brief pause. "If the cost is over fifty dollars, let me know, okay?"

"Of course," Evelyn said. "Hopefully most of the information will be free." Or almost free, such as the nominal charge for printing pages from the microfilmed plantation records. Evelyn made a note to herself to call Patricia in the morning and see if she'd located another copy of the missing microfilm. Although she seemed like a reliable sort, Evelyn's request might slip her mind.

"Do what you need to do, Evelyn," Abigail said. "I trust you."

Once again, Evelyn felt the weight of Abigail's faith in her. *Please, Lord, help me.* "Also, may I have your cell number? Then I can send you texts with questions or updates."

"Good idea." Abigail recited the number. "I hate to say this, but I really need to go."

"I'll keep you posted," Evelyn said. "And I'll be bringing my husband by for some of your fried chicken." James looked up from his work, brows raised in interest.

"Please do," Abigail said. "Have a good night."

After saying goodbye, Evelyn said to James, "As soon as I have something to show her, we'll go by Abigail's Kitchen and grab a bite." A dinner out would be a perfect reward for her efforts.

She had barely set her phone down when it rang again, a number she didn't recognize. At first she was going to decline it, but then she went ahead and answered.

"Evelyn? This is Cora Beth Bryant, from the Ezekiel Snow House."

Evelyn's ears perked up. Maybe the curator had information for her about Israel Gibbs. "Hey, Cora Beth. How are you?"

"Good, good. Listen, I was wondering how you made out at the heritage society? Were you able to find the plantation records?"

Evelyn sighed. "No, I'm afraid not. The ones I need are missing."

After a short silence, Cora Beth said, "Missing? You mean they didn't have the right ones?"

"No, I mean they're gone. The volunteer helping me was very surprised when she couldn't find the right box."

Cora Beth was quiet a moment. Then she said, "That is a setback then. What's next? Any idea?"

Evelyn was glad that Cora Beth seemed to be taking an interest, because earlier she'd been more annoyed than helpful. "Patricia is going to see where else she can get the records," she said. "And I've got other avenues to explore."

The curator fell silent again, and Evelyn got the distinct impression she was waiting to hear more. But Evelyn wasn't ready to share anything until her work was fruitful, since it was bad enough that Abigail was depending on her results. She didn't want to build up Cora Beth's hopes as well.

"I'm going to poke around some more, and then I'll get back to you," Evelyn said. "Thank you for checking in."

"Let me know if you need help," Cora Beth said. "I mean that sincerely. After our meeting, I got to thinking about it. If Israel Gibbs helped with the raid, he should be recognized along with the rest of Harriet's spy ring."

Evelyn's feelings warmed toward Cora Beth. It sounded like she regretted being so dismissive about and obstructive to Abigail's request to include Israel.

"I'm really glad to hear you say that," Evelyn said. "Right now I'm trying to piece his life together. Build a complete picture." She thought of her husband's advice, that trying every avenue might yield unexpected results.

"Sounds like you know what you're doing," Cora Beth said, a note of surprise in her voice. "If you want to, swing by the museum when I'm there. I didn't see Israel's name in my research about the scouts, but maybe you can dig into the sources I found. I might have missed something."

"Thanks for the offer," Evelyn said. Building off Cora Beth's work would definitely save her time.

"Anytime. This number is my cell. Give me a buzz, make sure I'm around."

"Thanks, Cora Beth." After hanging up, Evelyn sat for a moment thinking over the conversation.

James glanced up from his work. "What's going on?"

"The first call was with Abigail, as you probably guessed. And that was Cora Beth from the Ezekiel Snow House." Evelyn shook her head. "She said she's interested in helping, which is a real surprise. Last night it seemed like she hoped Abigail would go away."

"Maybe she reconsidered," James said. "She was probably leery of adding more work to the project, especially since the exhibition is opening soon, you said."

"In three weeks," Evelyn said. "But all she has to do is put up a picture of Israel, if Abigail has one. We can write up the descriptive text if she doesn't have time." She shook herself with a sigh. "I'll let you get back to work. I'm going to search the veteran lists and pension records."

Armed with Israel's information, Evelyn searched one index then another. Then she searched a second time before groaning in frustration. She had found one man named Israel Gibbs—in the Pennsylvania Infantry. But a soldier named Israel Gibbs from Charleston, South Carolina, was nowhere to be found.

Chapter Nine

"What is it, Evie?" James asked. "I can hear you moaning and groaning over there."

Rather than try to explain, Evelyn carried the tablet over to the desk. "I can't find Israel Gibbs listed as a veteran. I tried the Union Army first, since that's the side he was helping during the raid. Then I tried the Confederate Army, and he's not there either. And there are no pension records for him."

James took the tablet and studied the page while sitting back in his chair and swiveling. "Regarding pension records, he or his dependents might not have applied for some reason. But he should be listed as serving, if he was an official part of that mission."

"According to his own words, he was asked to help by Harriet Tubman herself," Evelyn said. "I'd say that was official."

James handed the tablet back to his wife. "I agree." His smile was rueful. "There's only one answer—keep digging."

He was right, although after the lost plantation records and this dead end, she was downright discouraged. "What if I can't prove he was a veteran? How am I going to break that news to Abigail? She and her family have been honoring Israel as a veteran forever." What if Israel's story was a deathbed fantasy, created to give meaning to a difficult life?

"It wouldn't be the first time a family history was embellished," James said. When Evelyn squawked in protest, he said, "Hold on, I'm not done yet. The point is, you need to stay neutral. Gather the facts and then make a determination."

"But what should I tell her right now?" Abigail would no doubt be upset and angry if Evelyn said Israel wasn't listed as a veteran. She might even blame *her*, as the proverbial messenger of bad news. People were touchy when it came to family reputations.

"I wouldn't tell her anything yet," James said. "It's too soon. Historical records are not always reliable. And to compound the situation, our country was a mess after the Civil War." Leaning forward, he tapped on his keyboard and brought up a website. "Listen to this. After the war, many men were missing, either killed in action or dying as prisoners of war. Clara Barton—who founded the American Red Cross—decided to help locate as many as she could. She got over sixty thousand requests for help and was able to locate only twenty thousand soldiers."

"What happened to the others?" Evelyn could scarcely get her mind around the idea that tens of thousands of soldiers had gone missing. Her heart hurt for their poor families.

"Sadly, we'll probably never know," James said. "But that situation should give you a little context about Israel's situation. He didn't go missing, but his contribution might well have slipped through the cracks."

"That makes total sense." A new determination heartened Evelyn. "I'm going to take your advice and keep going. If there are answers out there, I'll find them."

James patted her on the arm. "That's the spirit. Remember, when God closes a door, He often opens a window."

After a restless night, Evelyn was a little groggy, and the cloudy skies seemed to reinforce her somewhat gloomy outlook. "Coffee," she croaked as she stumbled into the kitchen, beelining toward the pot.

James glanced up from his phone with a smile and the wisdom not to comment on her disheveled appearance. She hadn't showered or styled her hair yet. "It's going to be wet the rest of the week," he said. "A tropical storm is approaching Florida."

Evelyn made a sound of dismay as she poured steaming coffee into a mug. "Odd for November." November was usually the driest month in Charleston, with the most rainfall occurring in the summer.

"Want me to drop you off?" James asked. "I have time."

Carrying her mug to the window, Evelyn looked out at the garden. A spatter of raindrops hit the glass, but the sprinkle was light, more a spritz than a downpour. "No, I'll walk. It'll be a chance to use my new umbrella." She'd bought a red plaid one that was so much fun. Her spirits perked up slightly when she thought of the perfect pin to wear, one shaped like cute little red rain boots.

"Good luck today," James said. "I hope your volunteer locates those plantation records."

Evelyn's shoulders sagged at this reminder of her failure. "I hope so too. Otherwise...I'm stumped." Her determination from the night before had leaked away with her troubled night. Doubts had assailed her, as well as a fear that she'd displayed pride when claiming a sure victory. Why had she *promised* success? Wanting it didn't make it so. Surely she'd learned that lesson by now, at her age.

"Try a different angle," James said. "Maybe Israel is mentioned in source material about the raid. Or in books or articles about Harriet Tubman. Or her papers."

Evelyn appreciated the suggestions, but right now the task felt overwhelming. She pictured herself sifting through endless websites and piles of documents. "If I didn't respect you before, I sure do now. Historical research is hard work."

"It can be," James acknowledged. "A real needle in a haystack. Sometimes it's only my stubbornness that keeps me going." He came over to the window and kissed her cheek. "You'll get there, Evie. I have every faith in you."

She put a hand to her cheek, touched by his supportive words. Their eyes met, and she couldn't hold back a smile. "I love you."

He kissed her again, this time on the lips. "And I love you. I hope you have a wonderful day." A gust of wind chose that moment to sweep through the backyard trees, tossing branches wildly. "In spite of the weather."

A short while later, Evelyn was walking to work, her jaunty umbrella open above her head. The rain was steadier now, but she stayed snug and dry. Plus the air temperature was warm, almost tropical. With every step, she felt her spirits lift. There was beauty to be found even on a rainy day. The flowers in window boxes looked neon bright, and the umbrellas and rain slickers of other pedestrians were cheerful splotches of color. At first she didn't see the pigeon flock, but then she spotted them huddled, cooing, under the lip of a fountain, their feathers almost iridescent.

Before entering the hospital, Evelyn shook off her umbrella and closed it. Then she tucked it under her arm and strode into the lobby. Joy should be at work by now, and Evelyn wanted to give her an update.

Joy's warm smile greeted Evelyn as she entered the gift shop. "Coffee?"

"You don't even need to ask," Evelyn said with a laugh. Following Joy into the back room, she unzipped her raincoat, took it off, and then placed it and the umbrella on a chair. She ran a hand through her bob, smoothing it into place.

"I talked to Anne last night," Joy said as she poured coffee. "She told me what happened at the bank." Joy had been at a dentist appointment the previous afternoon, so she had been out of the loop.

"Did she tell you I almost got caught snooping around?" Evelyn accepted the mug and took a sip. "The bank president came right up on me while I was looking at David Smith's desk."

"David Smith being Harley's undercover name, right?" Joy said in a whisper. "Wow. Did he figure out what you were doing?"

Evelyn shuddered at the thought. She could imagine a call being placed to the hospital administrator, complaining about the behavior of an employee. "I sure hope not. I was able to take a couple of pictures of the desktop, and Megan confirmed that a paperweight still sitting there belonged to Harley. It was a gift, she said."

The two women moved out into the main room, Joy straightening items on display as they went. "That sounds like a hasty exit to me. Anne also said that the police showed up?"

"Yes." Evelyn peeked through the big windows into the lobby. "I'm hoping we can find out more about that from Norm."

"I saw him earlier, on his rounds," Joy said. "He should be back by here soon."

"Here comes Anne." Evelyn smiled and waved as she spotted her friend.

After Anne breezed in and accepted a cup of coffee, Evelyn said, "Joy and I were just talking about the incident at the bank. But I have more updates."

"Oh, do tell," Anne said, making herself comfortable against the counter.

Evelyn sighed. "No good news, I'm afraid. I ran into a dead end at the heritage society. The roll of microfilm I needed was missing."

Joy's mouth dropped open. "You mean they didn't have it after all?"

"The volunteer said it was misplaced. Or stolen." The gloom she'd successfully pushed away during her walk attempted to make a comeback. "She's calling around for another copy."

"That's good," Anne said. "I doubt they only made one."

Her friend's remark made Evelyn feel a little more cheerful. She was right. And if she had to call all over the country, she'd find those records. "Cora Beth called me last night and offered to help, which I thought was nice."

Anne fiddled with a cute teddy bear. "I wonder what changed her tune." To Joy, she said, "Cora Beth got all fussed up about Abigail's request to include her great-great-great-grandpa in the exhibit."

"I think she didn't want the extra work," Evelyn said. "And you really can't blame her. Time is pretty short." She sighed again. "And getting shorter with every day that passes."

Her two friends were silent for a moment, and then Joy said, "Have faith, Evelyn. Maybe these obstacles are divine detours."

"Or divine dead ends," Evelyn said. "Thank you so much for your encouragement, ladies. You seem to know what I need every time."

Joy and Anne smiled at each other. "What are friends for?" Anne asked.

"Here comes Norm," Joy said. The elderly security guard was striding across the lobby straight toward the gift shop, whistling as his duty belt jingled.

"Hey, Norm," Anne greeted the guard. "How are you today?"

He stopped dead in the doorway with a big smile, gazing around the circle of friendly faces. "You ladies sure are a sight for sore eyes." He sniffed the air. "Got an extra cup of coffee, Joy?"

Joy swung into action. "For you, Norm, always." She knew how he liked his java and she soon returned, mug in hand.

Norm accepted the mug with thanks. "I was telling the wife about your coffee, Joy. She wants to order some for the holidays. You get it from Texas, right?"

Joy looked pleased. "I do. Rafael is a friend of mine, and he does such a great job. You're not the first person to inquire about ordering some of his beans."

Evelyn saw an opening. "Wasn't Rebekah Osborne interested too?" she asked. The police detective had been very impressed with Joy's coffee, she remembered, and Joy had given the detective Rafael's company information.

"She sure was." Joy flashed Evelyn a smile that told her she understood the gambit. "She orders it all the time now, she told me."

"Rebekah Osborne," Anne mused. "We saw her yesterday at Charleston City Trust, didn't we, Evelyn? She and Officer Williams came in as we were leaving."

"Yes," Evelyn said. "We did. And about that, Norm. Did you hear anything to indicate why the police were calling on Buford Martin, the bank president?"

Norm's eyes lit up. "Funny you should ask." Although Norm was retired from the police force, he enjoyed staying in touch with his former colleagues. And although he would never divulge anything that might jeopardize a case, he shared what he could. Evelyn had the feeling he liked keeping his hand in the game, so to speak.

"Go on," Evelyn said, eager to hear what he had to say.

Norm's response was to glance around then sidle a little closer. "This isn't public yet, but it will be. So keep it under your hats, all right?" The three women nodded solemnly.

"You can count on us," Joy said. "You know that." Norm had been instrumental more than once in helping them solve mysteries around the hospital.

Evelyn's chest tightened as she waited for Norm to go on. She was holding her breath, she realized.

"I don't know all the details of course, but I do know this…" He paused dramatically, obviously relishing the spotlight. "They uncovered some irregularities in the books. Possible embezzlement, they said."

A thrill of alarm shot through Evelyn, and judging by her friends' faces, they shared her concern. "Who was embezzling?" she asked in a whisper.

"No one I know, I hope," Anne added. "I've been going to that branch for years."

"They think it was an employee in cash management," Norm said. "Fellow by the name of David Smith." He said the name with emphasis. "Doesn't that sound like a fake name to you?" He shook his head. "Anyway, he's gone missing apparently, so the police are looking for him." His eyes sparkled with fervent interest. "They might even launch a full-scale manhunt."

To Evelyn, it felt as though Norm's announcement had siphoned all the air from the room. The police believed that David Smith was a suspected embezzler on the run. She thought of his sweet wife and baby, waiting with trust and hope for his return.

Her visceral response was a heartfelt, "No," uttered with every atom of her being, fists clenched so tight she was sure she'd leave nail prints in her palms.

Norm, who of course didn't know the connection between new mother Megan Brooks and an alleged felon named David Smith, nodded. "It's shocking, isn't it?" He pushed his cap back then straightened it. "According to Rufus, a friend of mine who works at the bank, he was well liked. A nice young fellow. New to town but already settling in nicely."

"Rufus," Anne said. "Is he the security guard? The older African American man?"

Norm nodded. "That's Rufus. He used to be on the force, like me." He chuckled. "I guess security guard is the second career of choice for us old-timers."

Evelyn mentally noted the name. They should go talk to Rufus and see what he knew about David Smith. She was also encouraged that the guard had liked the young man. Surely someone with a cop's instincts would have sensed if he was shady.

"You said he was new to town," Joy commented. "Do they know where he came from?"

"Not that I've heard," Norm said. "Rufus mentioned he was sent by a consulting company specializing in bank operations. He had certain expertise they needed."

Evelyn had been wondering how the FBI had set up David Smith's employment. They must have laid a lot of groundwork before sending the undercover agent in to what, find proof of wrongdoing? But now he was in trouble instead.

"I wonder where he's been staying," Anne said. "Just think, his landlord might have been harboring a criminal."

"Maybe he's still hiding out at home," Evelyn said. If only they knew where that was.

"Doubt it," Norm said. "I'm sure they went to his place already, looking for him. They'd have his address at the bank, don't forget." A hint of suspicion crossed Norm's craggy face at their questions, but then he appeared to shake it off. "I'm sure Rufus will keep me posted on what's happening." He drank his coffee in several swallows before handing the empty mug to Joy. "Now I'd best be moving on to my rounds. Thanks for the coffee."

"Anytime, Norm," Joy said. "You know that."

The three women watched as Norm left the gift shop. "I'm sorry I reacted like that," Evelyn said. "But I'm totally shocked."

Anne sipped her coffee slowly. "It's upsetting for sure. I wouldn't want to be the one to tell Megan."

"Me neither." Evelyn cringed at the thought. It would break the young mother's heart right in two.

"We're facing a decision, ladies," Joy said. "Should we continue helping Megan under the presumption that Harley is innocent? Or accept what the police think, that he's robbed the bank and run off?"

Indecision warred in Evelyn's chest, a fight between heart and head, between what they hoped was true and what others claimed. Then logic spoke. "I can't accept that he's guilty," she finally said. "I mean, he barely took this assignment. Megan said he was a last-minute substitute. Did he really have time to start embezzling? Would he even know how?"

"That's a good point," Anne said. "It's possible he's been framed."

"Plus it doesn't line up with his other actions," Evelyn said. "One day the man is buying his baby a stuffed turtle and the next he's a fugitive?"

Joy's expression darkened. "What if the real embezzler got wind of his investigation? Maybe Harley was kidnapped."

Evelyn's breath caught. "You mean..." She couldn't bring herself to voice her deepest fears. It was entirely possible that the young FBI agent had been the victim of foul play.

Chapter Ten

Joy reached out a hand. "Let's pray." The trio stood in a circle, heads bowed, while Joy thanked God and prayed for the little family torn apart by mysterious events. She also prayed for little Logan's health and development.

"That was beautiful," Evelyn said after she concluded with a fervent amen of agreement. "I needed the reminder to give thanks in all circumstances."

"We can all use it at times," Joy said. "It's so easy to get caught up in what we see and hear. To try to do things in our own strength."

Evelyn raised a hand. "Guilty as charged."

"That's because you're so competent," Joy said. "My husband was like that too, expert at everything he touched. He had to work hard to rely on God sometimes."

While she appreciated the compliment about her abilities, Evelyn accepted the whole truth of Joy's statement. No question that she was a doer with a tendency to charge ahead under her own steam. She needed to slow down and wait upon the Lord.

"You know what we should do next?" Anne asked. "Go see Rufus, the bank security guard, and ask him about David Smith."

"I had the same thought," Evelyn said. "It sounded like Rufus was surprised when David was accused of embezzlement. You'd think, as a former police officer, Rufus would have noticed if he was acting shady."

"I agree," Joy said. "Although some criminals are really good at hiding their true colors."

"Hopefully he'll have some insights for us," Anne said. "I don't know him well, but he's friendly and kind, a real gem."

"Want to go during lunch?" Evelyn asked. "I brought a sandwich today, so I'll eat at my desk either before or after." She glanced at the clock. "Right now I'd better scoot."

"Sounds like a plan," Anne said. "I'd better get going too. I'm supposed to deliver some bouquets."

Joy led the way to the cooler. "I've got them ready to go."

After rinsing her cup, Evelyn said goodbye to her friends and headed for her office. It was time to put her concerns about Harley and Israel aside and focus on her job.

Cliff and his helper were up on stepladders again, tinkering with the systems up in the ceiling. A new leak had erupted from the pipes and had trickled across the floor, thankfully toward the desks instead of the Vault.

Stacia, who was already at her desk, rolled her eyes. "We're having more problems. Luckily I got here early and found the leak. Water was spraying all over the place."

"Oh no, that's terrible," Evelyn said, deliberately keeping her tone even. She had to admit it, she was annoyed. What if the water had gotten into the Vault this time? Couldn't the workers perform their jobs properly, the way she strived to do?

In everything give thanks. The words of scripture floated through her mind and Evelyn laughed, an unexpected outburst that sparked joy in her heart. Why not? Grousing and grumping weren't going to fix the pipes. "Well, it could be worse. At least we can still work in here." What if the burst pipes had flooded the entire office? They might have lost their computers, plus the racks holding old paper records might have been soaked.

Stacia studied her boss with bemusement. "Wow. That's not the reaction I was expecting."

"It's not my natural one," Evelyn said as she settled at her desk. "Believe me. And anything else takes lots and lots of prayer." She switched on her computer then checked the files in her full in-box. "Looks like we're going to have a busy day." Another thing to be grateful for, since she couldn't ruminate or worry while engrossed in the tasks at hand. Her busy brain needed to take a break from trying to solve puzzles now and then.

"I'm going to make a deposit while we're here," Anne said. She and Evelyn had just entered the lobby of Charleston City Trust's downtown branch.

"Go ahead. I'll wait here." Evelyn watched as Anne crossed the shiny tile floor to the teller line, pulling out an envelope as she went. From her vantage point near the door, she glanced around the bank. Emily, the customer service rep, glanced up from her work and gave Evelyn a smile and a tentative wave. Evelyn returned the gesture.

Was she imagining it, or was the bank under a pall of tension? The tellers appeared solemn and kept glancing at each other. Behind them, two bank officers conferred in whispers, one holding an armload of files. The security guard she'd seen last time came sauntering through from the back, thumbs in his belt as he gazed around the lobby. By his appearance, she guessed this was Rufus, Norm's friend. Still standing in line, Anne gestured him over. After speaking to her, he nodded and then continued on his rounds, circling the lobby and then disappearing into the back.

Evelyn had read almost every brochure in a nearby rack by the time Anne rejoined her. "Whew. That took forever," her friend said, tucking her receipt into her handbag. "Sorry." She glanced over her shoulder. "Rufus should be here in a minute. He's going to take his break and come talk to us. Let's wait outside."

"What did you say to him?" Evelyn stuffed the pamphlet she was holding back into its slot and hastened to follow Anne.

"I told him my name and that Norm was a friend of mine. Of ours." Anne laughed as she pushed out the lobby door. "Guess what? Apparently Norm has been bragging to him about the 'ladies of Mercy,' as he calls us. He told Rufus that we're aces at solving mysteries."

Evelyn felt her mouth drop open. "Wow. Now that's a compliment."

"Isn't it?" Anne beamed, clearly pleased. "The mention of Norm and a request for his help was enough to get his attention. He also figured out that I didn't want to talk about it in the bank, hence the offer to take a break."

They drifted down the sidewalk a short distance, watching the bank entrance for the security guard. After a minute or two, his lean, wiry figure pushed through the lobby door. "Ladies. Good to see you."

"Rufus, this is my friend Evelyn," Anne said.

The guard extended a big, warm, calloused hand. "Nice to meet you, ma'am. Rufus Gibbs at your service."

Evelyn halted mid-shake. "Gibbs?" It couldn't be. Surely Gibbs was a common name... She asked anyway. "Any relation to Abigail Gibbs Johnson?"

Rufus broke into a big smile. "Any relation? I'm her uncle. Known that girl since she was knee high to a grasshopper." Bright interest shone in his eyes. "How do you know Abigail?"

"Besides her fantastic restaurant, you mean?" Evelyn said. "She goes to church with a good friend of ours. Shirley Bashore. I'm helping Abigail with a historical research project." And failing so far, but no need to mention that uncomfortable state of affairs.

"Oh yes." Rufus snapped his fingers. "The Israel Gibbs project. She said she had a real fine researcher helping with that." He cocked his head. "And that's you."

"That's me," Evelyn said.

"Will wonders never cease?" Rufus shook his head. "Want to take a little walk to the park? We can chat there."

The trio set off down the sidewalk, discussing inconsequential topics such as the weather and the upcoming Thanksgiving holiday while they walked. Now that the rain had stopped and the sun was breaking through the clouds, pedestrians thronged the sidewalks.

After a couple of blocks, they entered the park, a green space edged by a balustrade overlooking the harbor. With unspoken agreement, they made their way to a spot near a palm tree, out of the main flow of foot traffic.

"Thanks for taking time to talk to us," Anne said. "Especially since you don't know us from Adam."

"You're friends with Norm and that's good enough for me," Rufus said with a shrug. His gaze grew shrewd. "Does this have to do with our missing young man by any chance?"

"How did you know?" Evelyn put a hand to her chest. His perceptive guess had caught her by surprise, although it probably shouldn't have. Rufus was no doubt as insightful and intuitive as Norm. "Never mind. The short answer is, yes." She gnawed at her lip, uncertain how to explain their interest without betraying Megan. Her relationship to the missing David Smith wasn't Evelyn's secret to tell.

Before Evelyn could come up with an approach, Anne said, "We're in touch with his family, and we promised to help them locate him. Since they can't, um, get around right now, we're their boots on the ground so to speak."

Rufus rocked back on his heels in surprise. "How did that happen? He told me he didn't have any family around here."

"He doesn't." Evelyn had recovered. "They made the connection through the hospital. Contacted us for information." She clamped her lips shut, guessing that Rufus wouldn't pry further.

The older man rubbed his chin thoughtfully. "Hmm. I see. They don't have any idea where he is?"

"No, unfortunately," Evelyn said. "He stopped communicating with them last week. They don't even know where he was living. Only that he was working here, in Charleston."

Rufus made a hissing sound. "That doesn't sound good. At all. I keep asking myself, how could I be so wrong about someone? I had no idea that—" He broke off. "I can't discuss the details, you understand?"

"We sure do," Anne said. "We don't want any details, do we, Evelyn?"

Oh, Evelyn wanted details but not at the cost of Rufus's integrity, that was for sure. "Tell us whatever you feel comfortable discussing," Evelyn said. "Our goal isn't to solve any...any *alleged* crimes. It's to reunite David with his family."

The security guard fussed with his hat, pushing it back on his grizzled head then settling it again. "I don't know much, I'm afraid. David kind of kept things close to his vest. Wanted to hear about you, not talk about himself."

Which made perfect sense as an undercover agent. "Do you know where he was living?" Evelyn asked. "Maybe we could go by there, see if his landlord knows where he might be."

Rufus pursed his lips. "You'll only be following in the footsteps of the police. I'm sure that's the first place they went."

"Probably so," Anne said. "But at least we can tell his family that we were thorough."

"Good point." Rufus rubbed his chin again. "He didn't give me an exact address...but I do remember him talking to Emily about his digs." A burst of excitement lit his eyes. "Tradd Street. It was somewhere on Tradd Street."

Anne's expression was dubious. "That's a pretty high-rent district. If you can find a place to rent, that is."

Rufus rested his thumbs in his belt. "True. But some of those mansion owners rent out little apartments. Or their carriage houses. Anything to help pay the property tax."

Tradd Street narrowed their search down from the entire city to one street, but it was still daunting. *Help us, Lord*, Evelyn prayed. *Help us find Harley's home.*

"You've given us a place to start," Anne said. "Thank you."

"I wish I could be of more help," Rufus said. "I'm not privy to the personnel files or anything."

"And if you were, we wouldn't ask you to betray your employer," Evelyn said. "That's not how we roll." No matter how much they wanted to solve a mystery, Evelyn and her friends were determined to stay on the up-and-up.

The trio began to stroll through the park toward the street, leaving the waterfront behind. "So are you having any luck researching Israel Gibbs yet?" Rufus asked. "That amazing story of his has been passed down through the generations. I remember when I first heard about it, as a boy. I was so proud of him fighting for freedom like that."

Rather than give Rufus the discouraging update, Evelyn decided to take the opportunity to see what he might know. "I've read the document Israel dictated to Sabra," she said. "It was fascinating. But I'm looking for additional sources because the museum wants them." Which was true. "Did you ever see any?"

"Mostly I remember what she wrote," Rufus said. "But I think there were some old newspapers that talked about the raid. My great-grandmother had copies."

"Are those still around?" Evelyn asked, hopeful. But surely Abigail would have passed those along if they were.

Rufus winced. "I don't think so. When she died, they cleaned out her place, took just about everything to the dump. She was a collector, you might say. She had stacks and stacks of dusty old newspapers and magazines everywhere."

To Evelyn, that sounded like a trove, but many people didn't think the same way about old publications. "I haven't checked old newspapers yet," she said. "But thank you for that idea."

"Well, if you think of anything—a book, a specific article, even family papers or letters—will you let me know?" Evelyn asked.

"Of course I will," Rufus said. "It's time for Israel to get his due. And thank you for helping us. We appreciate it."

Rufus went back into the bank, and Anne and Evelyn returned to the hospital. After Anne parked her car they strolled through the garden, paying a visit to the Angel of Mercy statue on their way.

"Looking at the Angel always makes me feel more peaceful," Evelyn said. The beautiful statue smiled down at them as if bestowing calm and encouraging trust in God.

"Me too," Anne said. "Do you want to sit for a minute before we go in?" The sun was out in full strength now and in the shaded grove, the air was both sweet and warm.

"Sure." Evelyn smoothed her skirt and sat down after checking that the bench was dry. "I have a few more minutes."

The friends sat quietly on the bench, the only sounds the twittering of birds in the trees and passing traffic on nearby roads. Delicate fragrance from the tiny white flowers on a tea olive shrub drifted through the humid air. In every season, this garden featured something beautiful and blooming.

"I'm looking forward to Thanksgiving," Anne said. "Addie is going to help me make the pies this year."

"What fun," Evelyn said. "I've been experimenting with new dressing recipes. James didn't like the first one I tried."

Anne laughed. "Really? What was in it?"

Evelyn told her the ingredients, and Anne laughed again when she relayed how James had pushed aside the prunes. "Tonight I'm making wild rice with pecans and cranberries. To go with a supermarket chicken." She planned to swing by the store for a rotisserie bird later.

"Rice?" Anne wrinkled her nose. "Don't get me wrong, I like rice in some dishes. Risotto. Red beans and rice. But not in my dressing."

Evelyn sighed. Another diner set in her ways. "Don't worry. I'll make my old standby too, corn bread dressing. I thought it would be fun to try something new, that's all."

Anne patted her hand. "You're right, it is fun to branch out and try something different." A mischievous smile hovered on her lips. "That's why I'm making walnut pie instead of pecan, I decided."

"What?" Evelyn jumped in her seat. "You can't. Pecan pie is a tradition."

"Bingo." Anne pointed a finger at her. "Don't mess with tradition, Evelyn. But if the rice is good, make a side dish of it, okay?"

It looked like she would be dressing that bird with corn bread again this year. But she could still experiment with new recipes, right?

Two men appeared at the far side of the garden, pausing to speak under the shade of a live oak. Evelyn elbowed Anne. "Look. It's Buford Martin." She didn't recognize the other man, who was tall and distinguished, his dark hair touched with silver. He wore a sleek goatee.

Anne's eyes narrowed. "He looks familiar to me. But I can't remember where I've seen him before."

Well, whoever he was, Buford Martin wasn't happy with him. While Evelyn watched, the bank president's face reddened and his fists clenched down by his sides. Then he raised his arm, as if to strike the other man.

Chapter Eleven

EVELYN LEAPED TO HER FEET, although what she could do if two men started to fight, she had no idea. She stared in horror as the banker's arm went back as if to throw a punch. But the other man didn't appear bothered at all. His hand flashed up, and he grabbed Buford's forearm.

"Cut it out." The angry whisper carried through the garden. "We're in public here. Anyone could come along and see you acting like a fool."

Buford glanced around, and Evelyn shrank back, hoping she and Anne were hidden by the bushes flanking their bench. Seeming not to notice them, he tugged his arm away from his companion's grip then smoothed his jacket sleeve.

"Playing the blame game won't work," the other man said, his voice at normal volume. "We need to play the hand we've been dealt."

"But Preston." Buford's tone was a whine. "Everything I have is at risk." He pulled out a handkerchief and mopped his brow. "A legacy of over two hundred years."

Anne's lips moved as she said the name silently. Then her brows rose, and Evelyn knew she'd realized who he was.

Preston snorted. "You and your legacy. That and fifty cents will buy you a cup of coffee. Wait. Let me restate that. Make it three bucks. Coffee sure is pricy these days."

"Whatever," Buford said. "I've got to go. I'm late for a meeting."

The two men strode off in different directions. Thankfully neither walked past where Evelyn and Anne were sitting.

"Wow," Evelyn said. "That was intense. I was about ready to call 911." She pictured the police arriving and separating Buford and Preston, as if they were still frat boys.

Anne was searching on her phone. "At least they were in a good spot if they needed medical attention," she said.

A gust of laughter surprised Evelyn, and she leaned back and let herself go. Anne glanced at her with surprise then joined in. After a minute, Anne swiped a finger under her eyes to collect the tears. "I needed that," she said. She held up her phone. "I did recognize him. That's Preston Snow, Lavinia Snow's son. You remember Lavinia from the museum?"

Evelyn nodded. "Of course. The Snows used to own that house too, right? They must have donated it, which is quite a gift when you think about it."

"It sure is, considering the price of real estate on Tradd." Anne scanned the page then said, "Preston runs the family business, Lowcountry Imports, according to the chamber website. He took over for his father, who died ten years ago. Lowcountry is a major importer of consumer goods from around the world, with warehouses in Charleston and Savannah." She tapped her screen. "According to the Lowcountry site, the company has been around since the 1800s. They used to import goods from Europe. And export local crops like rice and cotton in return."

"Hmm," Evelyn said, "I wonder if some Gibbs rice went out on those ships. The history here never ceases to amaze me, how connected everyone is."

"Tell me about it," Anne said. "One reason to be careful about what you say. You never know who's a cousin several times removed."

"I wonder if Preston's company banks with Buford," Evelyn said. "They're obviously friends—well, frenemies. And Lavinia pals around with Buford's wife, Mary Lou."

Anne grunted. "If Preston does have accounts at Charleston City, there's no way for me to look that up. But I do wonder what they were arguing about."

"It must have something to do with the embezzlement," Evelyn said. "I'm sure that's putting a lot of pressure on Buford. Once word gets out, he might lose a lot of customers."

"You're right," Anne said. "We don't have a lot of money in there, but I'd sure hate to lose it. And Addie's account too. Though I suppose the accounts are insured by the FDIC."

"Maybe you should move your money now," Evelyn said. "Whatever's going on, I'm not impressed with Buford and his bank at all."

There was a real possibility that Megan's husband was innocent, which meant he was being set up as the fall guy for the embezzlement. Maybe that was why he had taken off. But as always, the question remained—why hadn't he contacted Megan to let her know he was all right? Either he couldn't, which was a horrible thought, or he thought she was safer if he didn't get in touch.

Evelyn preferred to believe the latter. She glanced at her phone for the time. "Want to pop up and see Megan? I want to check on how she's doing."

"Love to," Anne said, falling into step with Evelyn. "Last night Addie was asking me if we could get Logan a gift. She can't wait to meet him."

"Aw, that is so sweet." Evelyn thought about baby gifts. She'd check with Megan and see what Logan needed, she decided.

"I love shopping for babies," Anne said. "Especially clothes. Those precious little dresses and pants."

"Let's go soon," Evelyn said. "After we see what Megan suggests."

"I was going to mention that," Anne said.

At the birthing unit, the guard nodded them through, and to Evelyn's delight, they found Joy and Shirley already visiting Megan, who was finishing up her lunch. A chorus of hellos greeted them. In the background, the television burbled quietly, set to a local station.

Anne smiled at Megan. "We'd like to buy a little something for Logan."

"So please tell us what you need," Evelyn said. "I mean, you weren't prepared for the birth, so you didn't bring any baby supplies. Am I right?"

"You are, but you don't need to give us anything," Megan said, though her glistening eyes revealed her pleasure at the idea.

"But we want to," Shirley said. "So don't even think about discouraging us." Her hearty laugh rang out. "We're all dying to do some shopping for that little peanut."

"Well in that case," Megan said. She set her spoon on the tray and picked up a wrapped brownie for dessert. "There are a few things we need that the hospital won't provide for the trip home."

"Hold on," Evelyn said, rooting in her bag. "I'll get my notebook." She dug out a pen and flipped the notebook open to a fresh page. She wrote *For Logan* across the top.

Megan named some basic baby supplies—onesies, a blanket, wipes, diapers. Then she gasped. "A car seat. I'm going to need one for when we go home. The one I bought is sitting in Boston, of course."

"I know just the place to buy one," Anne said. "Let me know when you want to go."

"Thanks. I'll take you up on that," Megan said. She glanced out the window. "I'll be glad when I can be out and about again. And when I can take Logan for a walk."

"Soon," Shirley said. "He's getting there."

Evelyn was dreaming of the cute little outfit she would pick out, along with a sweet, soft toy like the little turtle. It was sitting on the window ledge near her bouquet of flowers—which was holding up nicely, she was glad to see. She plucked a couple of dead leaves off the stems then did the same for another showy bouquet.

Megan gasped loudly, and when Evelyn turned to look, she saw her pointing at the television. "Turn that up, please."

Shirley grabbed the remote and raised the volume. To Evelyn's horror, she saw a familiar face on the screen. David Smith's headshot from the bank website, with a banner reading, BREAKING NEWS below.

"Police are on the lookout for David Smith," local newscaster Bailey Carver said. "Smith is a former employee of Charleston City Trust. He's wanted in connection with an inquiry into irregularities discovered during a bank audit."

Megan's face had gone pale, and her lips were trembling. "What does this mean? Do they actually think my husband *stole* from the bank?"

Oh no. Evelyn hadn't wanted Megan to find out about the investigation this way, with no preparation or warning. The shock must be terrible. But before she could say anything, footsteps sounded in the corridor, headed toward them.

Carson Lewis appeared in the doorway but, seeing the crowd gathered in the room, stopped short. "I'm sorry. I hope I'm not interrupting anything."

"No, not really," Evelyn said. "We were talking about gifts for the baby." Did he have news for Megan about Harley? Had her husband been arrested? She studied the FBI agent's expression for clues. But his calm demeanor didn't give anything away.

"Carson, what's going on?" Megan's voice was choked. She pointed at the television. "I just saw a story about Harley. They said he's suspected of 'irregularities' at the bank."

The agent's face grew somber. "So the story is out already. I was hoping they'd wait until I could locate him, bring him in. Handle it that way."

Evelyn stifled a gasp. That sounded as if the FBI now definitely believed that Harley was a criminal. During his earlier visit, Carson said that Harley might have gone into hiding, in fear for his life. He'd suggested that Harley could have gone rogue but wasn't totally sure.

"You aren't going along with the bank's accusations, are you?" Megan asked. "They're probably covering up their own crimes by blaming him."

"I've had a hard time with the situation as well," Carson said. "I worked with Harley for years. But the case we were working on involved big money." He shook his head. "He wouldn't be the first to have his head turned."

"No," Megan cried. "I know my husband. He'd never do something like that."

Anne gestured to the others, indicating they should slip out and give Megan and Carson privacy. As Evelyn left the room, she glanced back at Megan, who was crying. Whatever the truth was, Evelyn knew this much—she'd keep praying for this young mother and her little family.

Chapter Twelve

"Another day, another dollar," Stacia announced at closing time. She gathered her things. "What are your plans this evening?"

"Nothing too exciting," Evelyn said. "I'm going to make a wild rice dressing to go with rotisserie chicken." Since James had the car, she would stop by a small local market to buy ingredients.

Stacia's expression informed Evelyn what she thought of these admittedly dull plans. "I'm going out with some girlfriends to trivia night. Hopefully there will be some cute guys there."

"That sounds fun." Evelyn was glad that her dating days were long over. Her phone beeped with a new text from James, saying he would be late due to an unexpected department meeting. No problem. That would give her a couple of extra hours this afternoon. "Oh, and I'm going to dig into a historical research project too."

"Good times," Stacia said, breezing toward the door. "See you tomorrow."

"Have fun tonight," Evelyn called absently. If Cora Beth was at the Ezekiel Snow House, she could go by there on the way home. It was only a block or two out of the way. She reached for the phone. But first she was going to check in with Patricia Cooper.

Fortunately, Patricia was working at the heritage society. "Evelyn," she said cheerfully. "I was about to give you a call. Good news. I've found a copy of those records."

Evelyn slumped back in her seat with relief. "Really? That's great. Where are they?"

Patricia hummed a little. "Here's the not-so-good news. They're at a historical society over in Colleton County, near the headwaters of the Combahee." She named the town, which was located about an hour west out Route 17, deep in the countryside. A pleasant journey if not a convenient one.

"They won't let you borrow them?" Evelyn asked. "Through interlibrary loan?"

"I'm afraid not." Patricia sounded regretful. "I tried. But they don't want to let any microfilm leave the building." She sighed. "After what happened here, I don't blame them. I've scoured the whole place and haven't found that roll yet."

Evelyn didn't blame the organization either, but it was worth asking. "Thanks for tracking those records down. I'll give them a call, and maybe I can head out later this week." She wouldn't be able to drive out there until Saturday unless they had evening hours.

Patricia gave her the name of the organization, along with the phone number and contact name. "Good luck," she said. "And please, come back and visit us. We have lots of great resources."

"I will, Patricia. Thanks again." Evelyn disconnected then dialed Cora Beth, who said to come right over, she'd be there. At least Tradd Street was within reach today.

One thing Evelyn enjoyed about walking was the opportunity to really study buildings as she went past. In the historic district, there was plenty to admire. Gracious porches. Columns topped with scrolls. Inviting arched windows. Vines tumbling over ancient brick walls set with gates.

She was studying Lavinia Snow's elegant home when a slowing automobile startled her. Realizing she was blocking the drive, Evelyn hopped out of the way. A gold sedan with rental stickers pulled through the open gate, moving slowly enough that Evelyn clearly saw the driver.

Carson Lewis—again. What was he doing here?

A thought struck her. Rufus had said that David Smith was staying on Tradd Street somewhere. Could he have been staying here, on the Snow property?

Evelyn found herself rooted in place as Carson drove to the rear of the property, where he parked between another vehicle and a carriage house. As the FBI agent climbed out of the sedan, Preston Snow came down the veranda steps, waving a greeting.

Her pulse racing, Evelyn pressed close to the thick camellia bushes lining the drive. This visit had to mean something. Maybe Preston banked at Charleston City Trust, she mused, thinking of his earlier confrontation with Buford Martin. Perhaps Carson was picking up the investigation into the bank where Harley had left off.

Hoping the men wouldn't notice her, Evelyn continued to watch as Carson and Preston spoke briefly then turned in unison and went to the carriage house. There, Preston unlocked the front door and stood back to let his guest enter first.

Evelyn glanced around. No cars or pedestrians were passing, and all was quiet in the main house, so she tiptoed down the driveway. Still hugging the bushes, she stopped about halfway down, close enough to observe what was going on in the carriage house. Preston had switched on an overhead light, which allowed her to easily see the interior through the picture window.

The two men appeared to be searching the place, judging by the way Carson was pulling cushions off a sofa and Preston was opening and shutting cupboard doors. What were they looking for?

Sofa cushion in hand, Carson glanced out the window in her direction. *Uh-oh.* Evelyn dove into the shrubbery and landed against a prickly holly bush. Ouch. After detaching her sweater from the clinging leaves, she pushed through the bushes toward the street. Time to get out of here. When she reached the wall, she nipped out onto the drive and dashed around the corner onto the sidewalk. Then she ran down the sidewalk to her destination, the Ezekiel Snow House.

Before going inside, Evelyn took a moment to calm down, to breathe deeply and slow her hammering heart. She wasn't cut out for this cloak-and-dagger stuff, that was for sure. Once she was breathing easier, she grabbed the brass door handle of the Ezekiel Snow House and went inside.

In the exhibit room, Cora Beth stood near an open exhibit case while Lavinia Snow looked on. When Evelyn drew closer, she saw that the curator was arranging several brass antiques on a shelf.

The two women glanced up as she approached. "Hey, Evelyn," Cora Beth said. "I'll be with you in a minute."

"What are those?" Evelyn asked, curious about the display pieces.

Cora Beth pointed to each item in turn. "A salinometer jug, used to gauge how saline the water was before it went into the steam engines. A candle lantern from an army ship. And this is a megaphone we believe was used during the raid."

"Really?" Evelyn was fascinated. She pictured Israel or one of the other men shouting out for those escaping to come aboard.

"You've done a nice job, darlin'," Lavinia said. Clasping her hands together, she gazed around the room. "Everything looks beautiful."

Evelyn agreed that the exhibit had been laid out in an attractive fashion, with intriguing artifacts placed to catch the eye.

"Thank you, Lavinia." Cora Beth gave the older woman a hug. "You take care, you hear? I'm sure everything will go fine tomorrow."

Lavinia's brow wrinkled, distress in her eyes. "I sure hope so. I hate having surgery."

Evelyn hung back, hovering near the glass case. It wasn't her business why Lavinia was seeking medical treatment.

But in this case she couldn't avoid overhearing when Lavinia went on. "I've been putting off taking care of my bunions long as I could. The doctor straight up told me he'd have to fuse my bones if I didn't have it done now." Both Lavinia and Cora Beth glanced down at the older woman's feet. She was wearing flat white sneakers, Evelyn noticed, quite a contrast to the rest of her outfit, which was a designer suit and handbag.

Come to think of it, that was the same ugly pea-green handbag she'd had the other night. And the emblem that Evelyn had thought was loose was now gone entirely. They certainly didn't make expensive accessories the way they used to.

"You'll be fine," Cora Beth said. "In and out, home before you know it."

Lavinia shook her head. "No, I'm afraid not. The doctor said he's keeping me overnight at Mercy." She patted her chest. "Last time I had anesthesia, I got pneumonia. He doesn't want to take any chances."

Evelyn couldn't help but offer reassurance to the worried woman. "Excuse me for eavesdropping," she said, "but I work at Mercy, and we'll take really good care of you, I promise."

Lavinia's worried expression softened a little. "That does make me feel somewhat better, Ms...?"

Evelyn smiled. "I'm Evelyn Perry. I work in medical records."

"Oh." Lavinia nodded. "That's an important job."

"It is," Evelyn said. "But more important, the doctors and nurses at Mercy are all excellent."

"They really are," Cora Beth agreed. "We're all proud of Mercy, here in Charleston."

"Keep an eye out for me, Evelyn." Lavinia curled her fingers into claws. "I'll be the one clinging to the gurney for dear life as they wheel me down the hall."

Cora Beth's laugh pealed out. "Oh, Lavinia, you crack me up."

"Better to laugh than to cry, I always say." Lavinia began to hobble toward the door. "Now I'm going to go home and see what Preston's up to. He told me he doesn't want to rent out the carriage house again." She sighed heavily. "Even though it gives me a nice little cushion every month."

Once again, Evelyn shamelessly listened in. She was dying to ask questions, but thankfully Cora Beth did that for her.

"What happened to your tenant?" Cora Beth asked. "I thought you liked him."

"I did. I do. David was a real sweetheart. Or so I thought." Lavinia's eyes shone with disappointment. "Buford Martin even gave him a reference. You know, Mary Lou's husband. But he just up and disappeared last week. Here one day, gone the next."

Cora Beth sucked in a breath. "Without paying the rent? Did he owe you a lot?"

"No, no." Lavinia shook her head. "He was all paid up for this month. But he just left without saying goodbye." Her lips pushed out in a pout. "I hope it wasn't something I said."

"Oh, Lavinia." Cora Beth ushered her friend toward the entrance hall. "That's ridiculous. I'm sure it had nothing to do with you. Let me walk you out."

Evelyn was quite sure of that as well. David Smith's disappearance had been related to his job, not his landlady. Going by what Lavinia had said, she was as shocked as anyone that her tenant had run off. Either he was great at pulling the wool over people's eyes or he was innocent. Evelyn knew which she hoped to be true.

The front door shut, and Cora Beth came back into the room. She pushed her cardigan sleeves up. "So, where were we?"

Had she actually forgotten why Evelyn was here? "You were going to show me some research sources," Evelyn said. "To help me learn more about the raid and hopefully Israel Gibbs's role."

"That's right. That's right." Cora Beth stopped to straighten a picture frame. She gazed around, humming, before gesturing for

Evelyn to join her. Once they were both standing in front of the wall display, Cora Beth said, "I found a lot of detail in newspapers and magazines reporting the raid." She pointed to quotes, which listed the source. "The story went viral, you might say. It was published in newspapers as far north as Vermont. Plus in national magazines like *Harper's Weekly*."

Evelyn took quick pictures of the exhibit labels, figuring that was easier than taking notes. "Where can I find these publications?"

"The main branch of the local library has an extensive archive," Cora Beth said. "You have to make an appointment, though," she warned. "They keep a pretty tight rein on the materials."

Unlike the heritage center, Evelyn thought. "All right, I'll do that. Thanks." She thought of another question. "What do you do if you want to search in general for information about someone? If you don't have specific dates?" She wanted to see what else she could learn about Israel Gibbs.

Cora Beth looked pleased that Evelyn was asking for advice. "There are indexes you can search," she said. "There are also periodical guides for magazines and journals."

"Good to know," Evelyn said. "I've used those before but not for such old publications."

"They're available, fortunately. By the way, how's it going?" Cora Beth asked. "Any luck finding the Gibbs plantation records?"

Evelyn was glad to have progress to report. "Actually, yes. Patricia Cooper, the volunteer at the heritage society, located them at an organization in Colleton County. I'm going to drive out there sometime this week."

Cora Beth turned to tweak another picture frame into place. "That's good. Which organization is it?"

"Combahee River Heritage Society," Evelyn said. "In Jacksonboro."

Cora Beth nodded. "Perfect. They had some great Low Country life exhibits on display last time I went."

"Good to know," Evelyn said. She enjoyed poking around small museums, so she'd plan to spend a little time there after doing her research. She tucked her phone into her handbag. "Thanks for your help. I'll let you get back to work."

Cora Beth muttered a soft goodbye, her mind obviously already on her next task.

As Evelyn left the Ezekiel Snow House, she took out her phone again to bring up the grocery list. She'd just remembered that they needed milk and if she didn't make a note, she'd probably forget.

Wham. Evelyn banged into something, barking her shin. Looking down, she saw that several recycling bins were lined up along the sidewalk in front of Lavinia's house. They hadn't been there before or she would have known to avoid them.

Recycling bins. Did they hold trash from the carriage house? Maybe Carson and Preston had taken the opportunity to clean while searching for who knew what.

Evelyn peered into the tubs, organized by type. One held cans, another glass containers, and the third, paper. Mostly newspapers, it looked like, with a couple of local tourist publications thrown in.

But on top was a takeout menu for A.J.'s Roadhouse. The restaurant name sounded familiar, and after a few seconds, she remembered where she'd heard it. Stacia had gone there on a date a few days ago. It was down by the waterfront, she'd said. Good pizza.

A.J.'s probably wasn't the kind of place Lavinia or Preston Snow frequented. They were more likely to dine at the Charleston Grill or Revival.

Harley must have eaten there. Or gotten takeout. Evelyn glanced down the driveway. Carson's sedan was still there, but the backyard was empty. Hoping no one witnessed her poking through the trash, Evelyn grabbed the menu and tucked it into her handbag. One never knew where a clue might lead, right?

Evelyn strode down the sidewalk, her mind ticking over the events of the afternoon. Carson searching the carriage house meant what, exactly? That the FBI was officially investigating the embezzlement? Had Carson found anything to help them locate the missing man? Surely the FBI wouldn't reveal David Smith's true identity to the bank they had been investigating. Although they might know, if Harley had turned.

It was all a mystery, but there was one thing Evelyn was pretty sure of. Something had gone terribly, terribly wrong.

"Yoo-hoo. Evelyn. Is that you?"

A woman calling out gradually penetrated the fog in Evelyn's mind. She stopped walking and looked around.

"I'm over here. In the garden." Behind a wrought iron fence, a woman rose to her feet, removing her gardening gloves. She wore a wide-brimmed hat that shaded her features plus a pair of sunglasses.

As Evelyn continued to stare, she pushed up the glasses. "It's me. Mary Lou Martin." She gave a little laugh. "I'm not surprised you didn't recognize me under all my protective gear." She patted one soft pale cheek. "But Momma always told me to keep my face out of the sun."

"Oh hello, Mary Lou." Evelyn glanced up at the tan clapboard house with its double porches and white trim. She hadn't known that the Martins lived on this street, but it wasn't entirely surprising. They were among the Charleston elite. "I love your house."

Mary Lou stared up at the facade. "It's been in my family forever. I feel so privileged to live here."

"I feel the same way about my house on Short Street," Evelyn said. "But my family has only lived there for fifty years."

"Still special, though, am I right?" Mary Lou gestured toward the house. "Can I interest you in a glass of sweet tea?"

Evelyn studied the other woman. Why was she being so friendly? When Evelyn had met her at the Ezekiel Snow House, Mary Lou had been cold and standoffish. But ever charitable, Evelyn decided to give her the benefit of the doubt.

"I'd love a glass," she said, mentally rearranging her schedule. Her plan to buy a cooked chicken gave her a little wiggle room. Maybe she could buy some prepared potato salad as well. The market had tasty choices in the deli case. Then dinner would be a snap to prepare.

At Mary Lou's gesture, Evelyn followed her hostess onto the porch. She settled in a white wicker peacock chair while Mary Lou went inside for their tea. Evelyn sat back against the soft cushions, enjoying her view of the garden, which featured an ancient oak tree and a variety of roses. Joy would love to see them, she knew, although it looked as if the oak tree was dying.

Thinking of her friend, she pulled out her phone and sent a quick text. WE NEED TO TALK. SO MUCH TO TELL YOU! She also snapped and sent a picture. SITTING ON A TRADD STREET VERANDA.

Joy texted right back with exclamations. CAN'T WAIT TO HEAR!!!

Evelyn had another idea. Why not invite Joy to dinner? Although she was often busy with her daughter and grandchildren, Joy spent a lot of time alone. Contentedly to be sure, usually working in her garden, but still. That way she could give Joy and James all her updates at the same time. She dashed off the note.

Joy accepted immediately. I'LL ENJOY EATING SOMEONE ELSE'S COOKING FOR A CHANGE, LOL. THANK YOU.

Well, with half the meal prepared by the grocery, it wasn't quite home cooking, but it would do.

"Here we are." Holding a tray, Mary Lou emerged onto the porch, allowing the screen door to snap shut behind her. She set the tray on a low table. Besides two tall frosty glasses of tea, there was a plate of lemon cookies. "Help yourself."

Evelyn took a glass of tea and a cookie, plus a napkin. "Thank you, ma'am."

"You're welcome." Mary Lou picked up the other glass and sat down in the adjacent chair with a sigh. "Sitting feels so good. Getting old, I guess. My knees are creaking."

Evelyn guessed Mary Lou was a little older than her, mid-sixties, probably. "I refuse to accept my age," she said. "I'm in outright denial."

Mary Lou's gaze traveled over Evelyn, landing on her face. "You look great. So it must be working." She sipped her tea, ice cubes rattling.

"Good genes, mostly," Evelyn said. She gestured to the yard. "Your gardens are lovely."

"Thank you. I'm quite proud of them, I have to admit." Mary Lou sat up a little straighter. "I've been restoring them to their original splendor, from old garden plans I came across in the attic."

"What a find," Evelyn said. She supposed the attic of a house this age, in the same family since it was built, must hold a veritable trove.

"The place is absolutely stuffed," Mary Lou said. "But whenever I resolve to clean it out, I come across something special. Now I don't dare get rid of anything."

"I'd leave it all in place if it were mine," Evelyn said. "It's like a timeline of your family's history up there."

"A dusty timeline," Mary Lou said. "But yes, you're right." She seemed to think about something, and then with resolve she set her glass on the table. "Want to see the garden plans? I had them framed."

If it meant getting inside that house, then yes. Evelyn set her own glass down and followed Mary Lou. Like the Ezekiel Snow House, Mary Lou's home still had vintage charm. So many historic houses had been renovated to the point of making them modern and often charmless.

A carved staircase curved up at one side of the foyer, which had a black-and-white marble floor. Fresh flowers sat on a tall antique piecrust table under a crystal chandelier. Pocket doors stood open on the left, providing a glimpse of a gracious double parlor within.

"What a gorgeous home," Evelyn said in admiration as they walked through the foyer into the parlor.

Mary Lou smiled in acknowledgment. "We've done some updates, especially in the kitchen and baths, but everything else is pretty much original." She patted the glossy wood of a tall armoire. "Including most of the furniture."

What must it be like to live with precious antiques? Evelyn wondered. She'd probably be afraid to do anything, especially eat or drink.

Her hostess halted in front of a wall holding numerous paintings, prints, and photographs, including a portrait of a beautiful woman holding a fan and sitting on a veranda. She reminded Evelyn of Vivien Leigh in *Gone with the Wind*. A gold label on the frame read, PORTRAIT OF BELINDA SNOW GIBBS.

But Mary Lou was pointing to a large sepia-toned document. "This is it." The marks on it were faded and hard to read.

Evelyn stepped closer, squinting at the document. Gradually the illustration became clear—a footprint of the house and notations regarding suggested plants in the gardens.

"That's the same live oak," Mary Lou said with a laugh. "Believe it or not. But this magnolia is long gone." She pointed to both on the plan.

But Evelyn's attention wasn't on the trees. The handwritten script along the top had caught her eye. GARDEN PLAN FOR THE BENJAMIN GIBBS TOWN HOUSE.

Chapter Thirteen

Evelyn's inhale of breath must have been audible, because Mary Lou frowned at her. "I didn't know you were a Gibbs," Evelyn said. "Am I reading that right?" Not only was the banker's wife a Gibbs, she was a descendant of the very Benjamin Gibbs who had owned a rice plantation and hired Israel to run his crops down the river.

Mary Lou's nose went up in the air. "Gibbs was my maiden name. We're one of the *oldest* families in Charleston. One of the first to settle here. We're related to *everybody*."

"That's amazing," Evelyn said. "So much history." It was on the tip of her tongue to ask about Israel Gibbs, but she hesitated. Why hadn't Mary Lou come forward when Abigail had asked to include him? Maybe she didn't know any details about Israel or that he had been so closely tied to her ancestor.

"Have you had any luck?" Mary Lou asked.

Now it was Evelyn's turn to be confused. "What do you mean?"

Mary Lou turned and headed out of the room. "With your little project. Israel Gibbs."

"Some," Evelyn said. "Still tracking down sources." She decided to go ahead and ask the question weighing on her mind. "Do you know anything about his background? I've gathered that your ancestor hired him."

"That's what Abigail said." Mary Lou shook her head. "But I've never seen any proof."

That was an odd way to put it. Evelyn considered asking a few more questions, but she couldn't think quite how to pose them. Benjamin Gibbs had owned one of the plantations from which enslaved people were liberated, so it was awkward to say the least.

Mary Lou stopped walking. "If you're wondering," she said, her pale cheeks flaming, "I'm not proud of…of certain aspects of my family's past. I can't change it, but I do what I can to make a difference now." She lifted her chin. "It was my idea to hold the Harriet Tubman exhibit. To honor the brave souls who fought for freedom."

Evelyn's assumptions about Mary Lou underwent a rapid reshuffling. "It is a great exhibit," she said. "If you have any ideas how we can prove Israel was involved, will you let me know?"

Now the cold veil was back. "I don't have any information about that. Please don't press me any further."

A wave of heat flushed Evelyn's skin. Nothing like being put firmly in your place. She almost apologized but then held the words back. She hadn't done anything wrong or out of the ordinary. As a descendant of Israel's employer, Mary Lou was an obvious person to talk to.

By the time they reached the porch, Evelyn had decided she'd better get going. She couldn't imagine sitting on the porch and making small talk after that tense exchange. "Oh, will you look at the time?" she exclaimed. "It was so nice to see you, Mary Lou, but I must excuse myself."

Mary Lou, who was now sitting in her wicker chair, merely nodded. "Nice to see you too. Have a good evening."

"I will," Evelyn said as she gathered her handbag. "Thank you for the cold drink and your hospitality."

She practically ran down the steps and through the gate onto the sidewalk, conscious all the while of Mary Lou's eyes on her back.

Once she was down the block, the adrenaline ebbed and Evelyn slowed to catch her breath. What a strange encounter. She was practically dizzy from the changes in Mary Lou's moods. It was really too bad that Mary Lou didn't have—or want to look for—any family records related to Israel. Why was Mary Lou so unhelpful regarding Israel? There had to be a reason.

But the good thing was, there were other avenues to pursue.

"Joy. So glad you could make it." Evelyn stood back to let her friend walk into the house.

"I never say no when someone cooks for me," Joy replied with a laugh. She thrust a big bouquet of lilies and roses at Evelyn. "Here. Put these in water."

"Aren't you the sweetest thing?" Evelyn took the flowers, inhaling their fragrance. She led the way to the kitchen, where she found a vase.

"Something smells good," Joy said, setting her handbag on the island.

Evelyn turned on the tap, filling the vase with cool water. "Wild rice dressing. It's in the oven with the rotisserie chicken I'm warming up." She plunked the flowers in the vase then set it close to Joy for her expert touch.

Joy tweaked the flowers into place. "Tell me what I can do to help."

"Not much," Evelyn said. "I've already set the table." They were eating in the dining room tonight. She opened the oven door and peeked inside. "Maybe help me carry out the food when it's ready?"

"I can do that." Joy perched on a stool, resting her chin on her hand. "Your kitchen is gorgeous. Every time I come over I'm impressed all over again."

"James did a nice job," Evelyn said. "We really aggravated each other in the process, but I love it."

"So good to hear," James said as he swept into the room. "Hello, Joy. How are you?" He continued on and gave Evelyn a kiss. "Something smells good."

"That's what I said." Joy slid off her stool. "Is there tea in the fridge, Evelyn?"

"Yes." Evelyn slid her hands into oven mitts. "Sorry. I should have offered you something to drink."

"No problem." Joy dispensed ice into three glasses and filled them with tea. She handed one to James. "How's school going?"

"Great," James said, raising the glass in a salute of thanks. "But the students are already getting itchy for the holidays. Thanksgiving's coming right up, and then we come back for two weeks to finish the semester."

"I remember that feeling," Joy said. "The anticipation and relief of being almost done."

"Yeah, we professors experience it too," James said with a laugh. "What can I do to help?"

"Potato salad and cucumber salad are in the fridge," Evelyn said. "Can you put them on the table, please?"

James and Joy did as she asked while Evelyn carved the chicken, piling meat on a platter. Then the platter and the dish of dressing went to the dining room, along with full glasses of iced tea.

"Let's say grace." James bowed his head and the women followed suit, praying along with him. He lifted his head. "Let's eat."

"This isn't bad," James said a few minutes later, after sampling the wild rice dressing. "What's in it?"

"No prunes," Evelyn quipped. "Bacon, mushrooms, cranberries, and pecans."

Joy scooped up dressing along with chicken. "I like it. It's different."

"See?" Evelyn said to her husband. "I'm not the only one who likes to branch out once in a while."

Their guest looked confused so James clarified. "Evelyn is thinking of substituting this or another recipe for her usual corn bread dressing." He pulled a face. "I'm Team Corn Bread all the way."

Joy's mouth dropped open. "No corn bread dressing? Why that's a travesty. We always have corn bread dressing in Texas."

"Didn't I tell you, James?" Evelyn said. "After talking to Anne, I decided to do the corn bread for sure. But I'm also going to make a new recipe."

"The art of compromise," James said. "A perfect solution."

"What other recipes were you thinking of trying?" Joy asked.

"Just one more," Evelyn said. "An oyster dressing. With fresh South Carolina oysters, of course."

Joy served herself another scoop of cucumbers. "That sounds... different. Kind of old-fashioned."

"My grandmother used to make it, according to notes on the recipe," Evelyn said. "I feel such a connection to her when I leaf through her old cookbook."

"A good reason right there to try new recipes," James said. "Whatever you decide is fine by me."

"Thank you, dear," Evelyn said. "You're the cutest guinea pig ever."

James patted his trim midriff. "Maybe just a pig. Can you please pass me the potato salad, Joy?"

"So Evelyn," Joy said. "Tell me about that house on Tradd Street." To James, she said, "She sent me a picture of the loveliest garden this afternoon."

"That garden belongs to Mary Lou Martin," Evelyn said. "Yes, the banker's wife," she added in response to Joy's unspoken question. "And visiting her was only the tip of the iceberg. So much happened after I left work."

While they continued to eat, Evelyn took her dinner companions through her experiences on Tradd Street. Seeing Carson Lewis search the carriage house. Visiting the Ezekiel Snow House. Finding the menu. Drinking sweet tea with Mary Lou. "The biggest questions I have are"—she held up a finger—"one, did Carson find any clues to Harley's location, and two, what does Mary Lou Martin have against Israel Gibbs?"

James set down his fork. "It sounds like Carson stepped in to help the bank with the embezzlement case."

"Hopefully without revealing that David Smith was an undercover agent," Joy said. "Surely that would put Harley's life in danger. Unless he's working with the criminals."

"That's what Carson said today," Evelyn said. "Poor Megan. She was so upset."

"I'll bet." James's expression was somber. "Bad enough that your husband goes missing. And then to hear that he's involved in a crime? That's a real blow."

Evelyn thought back to the events of the afternoon. "Here's something that doesn't sit right," she said. "Preston Snow was helping Carson search the carriage house. Doesn't that seem fishy to you?"

Joy got it. "Because he's not in law enforcement? I agree. Yes, he's the landlord, but he should have let Carson in and then stayed outside."

"That is strange," James said, rubbing his beard. "Did Carson have a warrant?"

"I have no idea," Evelyn said. "I didn't see one." Maybe she had missed that part. Putting aside her speculations for now, she pushed back her chair and asked, "Who wants dessert?"

Evelyn and her friends were enjoying a cup of coffee in the gift shop the next morning when they had an unexpected visitor—Megan.

"Hi, everyone," the new mother said with a smile. She glanced down at her jeans and sneakers. "I'm in real clothes again." Instead of a maternity top, she wore a T-shirt from the gift shop depicting the Angel of Mercy statue. "Well, almost. Still have my stretch pants on."

"It will take a while for you to get down to your normal size," Anne said with a smile. "But don't worry, it'll happen." She sipped coffee. "Eventually."

Megan groaned. "I hope so."

"Do you want coffee, Megan?" Joy asked. "I have decaf by the cup."

"Thanks, I'd love some," Megan said. She wandered over to the stuffed toys and rotated the stand. "These are so cute. I want to buy another one for Logan." She smiled a thank-you when Joy handed her a mug.

Evelyn remembered the FBI agent's visit to the carriage house. "Megan, we figured out where Harley was staying."

Megan's head jerked up. "Really? Where?" Her fingers tightened around a toy narwhal.

"On Tradd Street," Evelyn said. "In Preston and Lavinia Snow's carriage house, which is now a rental. A security guard at the bank told us that David Smith had been renting somewhere on that street. Yesterday I figured out where, thanks to Carson. He pulled into the driveway when I was walking by, and then he and Preston went into the carriage house and started searching it. Not Carson alone, as you might expect. *Both* of them."

"That is strange," Shirley said. "Why would Carson have the property owner help?"

"He wouldn't. He couldn't be sure that Preston isn't involved, either in the embezzlement or David Smith's disappearance," Joy said.

"You're right, Joy," Megan said. "Harley told me how careful they have to be to maintain the chain of custody for evidence. I can't imagine why Carson did that," she added, her face a mask of doubt and confusion. "But did they find anything, Evelyn? Any clues to where my husband might be?"

"I don't know," Evelyn admitted. "I watched them for a few minutes but then skedaddled out of there. I was afraid Carson or Preston might catch me."

Anne's eyes were wide. "Oh, Evelyn. That was risky."

Evelyn chuckled ruefully. "I know. But I had to find out what they were doing." She took a sip of coffee. "I did find a takeout pizza menu in the trash when I came back by later. I wonder if Harley went there. My assistant, Stacia, goes to the same place."

"Harley loves pizza," Megan said. "We used to go out almost every week to our favorite place." Her voice was wistful.

"Hold on a minute," Shirley put in. "I'm still back on trash. Were you rooting through garbage cans, Evelyn?"

"No." Evelyn cringed at the thought. Would she have gone that far? "Recycling bins. The menu was sitting right on top. I couldn't help but notice it. After I ran into the bin and banged my shin." She glanced down at her slacks, which hid the bruise she'd discovered after her shower.

"Ouch." Anne winced. "I hate when that happens."

"We should go get pizza," Megan said, her eyes aglow. "Maybe someone there has seen my husband."

"I was thinking about doing that," Evelyn said. "But I don't think you should go to A.J.'s, Megan. We don't want anyone making a connection between you and David Smith. Better safe than sorry." A chill went through her at the thought. If Harley's cover hadn't been blown already, it might be if someone was savvy enough to connect Megan to his real identity. And if, by some chance, Harley had taken off with the bank's money, then someone might try to use Megan and Logan as leverage. As a newcomer to Charleston and the bank, Evelyn doubted Harley had been working alone.

Megan's face fell. "Yeah. I get it. But now that I'm recovered from giving birth, I feel like scouring every square inch of this city. It's hard sitting here and waiting. Doing nothing."

If James were missing, Evelyn would feel the exact same way. "I understand, Megan," she said. "I'm praying for a swift resolution to this situation." And a happy ending. Anything else was intolerable.

"You're not doing 'nothing,' as you put it," Shirley said fervently. "You're taking care of Logan. That little boy needs his mama."

As the other ladies chimed in with agreement, Evelyn glanced out into the lobby. She'd been keeping watch while they were talking to Megan, mindful that customers might enter at any moment. What they were discussing was far too sensitive for public consumption.

She saw an older woman headed straight toward the gift shop, which meant their conversation was over for now. She was limping, and as she got closer, Evelyn recognized Lavinia Snow. Ah, yes, she was scheduled for bunion surgery today. But why was she coming to the gift shop instead of checking in at the surgery unit?

As the older woman made her way slowly but steadily toward the shop, Evelyn shushed the others. "We've got company."

Anne peered out the window. "Lavinia Snow? What's she doing here?"

Mindful of patient privacy, Evelyn said, "I'll let her tell you that, if she wants." She waved as the newcomer hobbled through the doorway. "Hey, Lavinia."

"Evelyn. I thought that was you." Lavinia looked around the gift shop. "I decided to pick up a few magazines and some chocolate, for after my surgery. I haven't had a blessed thing since yesterday evening. Not even a glass of water."

"It's tough, I know," Shirley said, "but much safer."

"So they tell me," Lavinia grumbled. She continued across the shop, heading toward the magazine rack. Partway, she stopped to stare at Megan. "I'm sorry, but do I know you? You look familiar."

Chapter Fourteen

EVERYONE FROZE, ESPECIALLY MEGAN, WHO resembled a startled deer. Then, recovering, the young mother said, "I don't think I've had the pleasure." She held out her hand. "I'm Megan." *Smart to omit her last name,* Evelyn thought, since they didn't know if Harley's cover had been blown. It was possible that the Snows knew their tenant's real identity—maybe even from Carson.

The older woman took her hand and shook. "And I'm Lavinia. Here to get my bunion removed."

Megan shot Evelyn a questioning glance. Evelyn nodded, guessing she was asking if this was the same Lavinia they'd been talking about.

"Oh my," Megan said, her nose wrinkling up. "Does it hurt a lot?"

"It sure does," Lavinia said, indicating her foot. "But I've been so afraid of having surgery that I put it off." Fear shone in her eyes. "Last time I had anesthesia, I got pneumonia. My lungs weren't good anyway and now they're worse. I already get sick every winter. This might put me under."

Shirley stepped closer. "Who's your surgeon?" After Lavinia named her, Shirley said, "She does a great job. And so does our anesthesiologist. They'll be watching you closely."

"That's what my primary care doctor said." Lavinia's hands clasped together. "But I'm still scared."

Anne said, "Lavinia, I'm Anne, a volunteer here. Would you like us to pray for you?" When Lavinia looked doubtful, she added, "We do it all the time. Joy serves up coffee and prayers in this gift shop."

A small smile crept over Lavinia's tense features. "All right. I'd like that, if you don't mind."

"We don't mind." Anne's voice was firm. "Why don't we hold hands?"

The women moved closer together, each reaching out to take a neighbor's hand. Once they were ready, Anne prayed for the success of Lavinia's surgery, for her to experience a speedy healing and recovery, and for her lungs to be healed and healthy.

"That was beautiful," Lavinia said, blinking rapidly. "Thank you." Her eyes were damp with tears. She laughed. "Now I'd better get my magazines and scoot, before I'm late."

Evelyn checked the time. She still had a few minutes, so she lingered while Lavinia chose and paid for magazines and chocolate. Joining Megan at the carousel of toys, Evelyn helped the young mother decide which one to buy. The cute narwhal was the clear winner. Meanwhile, Shirley went back to the emergency room, and Anne took a delivery of flowers upstairs to a patient.

Megan's phone beeped. She pulled it out of her pocket and studied it with a frown. After reading for a moment, she gasped, clapping a hand over her mouth.

Lavinia gathered up her purchases. "I'll check back in tomorrow," she said. "Thanks again for everything."

"If you need anything, let us know," Joy called. "We deliver."

"I will," Lavinia said. She stopped and turned around. "When they send me a survey, I'm going to tell them how great you are here at the gift shop."

Joy smiled at her. "I appreciate that, Lavinia. Keep in touch."

Once Lavinia was gone, Evelyn turned to Megan. "She owns the carriage house your husband was renting."

"I thought so," Megan said. "Wow, she certainly gave me a start, saying I looked familiar."

"That was strange," Evelyn said. She changed the subject. "Not to be nosy, but did something happen? I noticed you got a message that startled you."

Megan nodded, turning the phone toward her. "My mother has been checking my mail while I'm out of town. There was another postcard today, in a package with a baby book about boats." Her eyes brimmed with tears. "From Harley."

Joy scooted around the counter and hurried over. "Wonderful news. What does the postcard say?"

Megan grimaced in frustration. "It's kind of strange." She enlarged the picture her mother had sent. The postcard depicted Mother Emmanuel Church. "He wrote"—she blinked rapidly, trying to hold back the tears—"'Sometimes you have to keep the faith.'" Her voice broke into a sob. "He's okay. I don't know where he is, but he's okay. And he's innocent. I just know it."

Relief swept over Evelyn. In the back of her mind, she'd been worried that Harley had run away, as some claimed, or worse, was dead.

Joy hugged Megan, cooing over her with comforting words. "I think he's still in Charleston. Why else send a postcard of that particular church?"

Megan pulled back slightly. "You're right. Did he buy that one in here?"

"No, we don't carry those," Joy said. "Though we should. Mother Emmanuel is one of our most magnificent landmarks."

Evelyn checked the time again. "Oops. I'd better go. Megan, I'll be up later to visit you and Logan."

"Please do," Megan said. "It gets lonely sometimes."

As Evelyn left the gift shop, she saw that Joy and Megan were deep in conversation. That made her happy. If anyone could soothe a person, it was Joy.

The maintenance men were in Evelyn's office when she arrived. "Good morning," she said. "I kind of feel like we're coworkers now."

Cliff laughed. "Sorry about that, ma'am. We'll be out of here soon. By Monday all will be back to normal."

"Good to hear," Evelyn said. That meant she had only today and tomorrow to get through before she could visit her beloved Vault again.

"I know it's been inconvenient," Cliff said. "But I'm telling you, we're not happy about how long it's taking either."

Slightly mollified, Evelyn said, "I know that. I appreciate your hard work." She settled at her desk. At least the leaks weren't affecting the actual records operation. Everyone needed medical records and they needed them now.

Stacia entered the office, taking off her coat as she walked in. "Sorry I'm late." She smiled at the maintenance workers. "Hi, guys. Want a coffee? I'm buying." They accepted her offer with big grins and thanks.

"I should have offered to do that," Evelyn said. "But I can help pay." She pulled out her wallet. "Want to get me one too? A small, please." Her nerves were already humming from the coffee she'd had so far this morning.

Stacia zipped back out of the office, money in hand. Before Evelyn started updating records, she took a moment to look up the Combahee River Heritage Society's hours. *Oh no.* They were closed this weekend, due to an event. But they were open late tonight, until seven. If she left right after work, she'd have an hour or two to poke around.

But James had the car... Evelyn sent Anne and Joy a text. Maybe one of them—or both—would go with her. They could grab something to eat on the road.

She had an idea. What if she and James went to Abigail's Kitchen on Friday night for dinner? Then she could give Abigail an update in person. After sending James a text about her plans, she called Abigail.

"Hello, Evelyn," Abigail said. "I've been meaning to get in touch. Are you having any luck?"

"To be honest, I've had a setback or two," Evelyn said. "But I'm on the trail now. Heading out to Colleton County to look at their archives."

"Colleton County? Girl, you're going the extra mile. Literally." Abigail laughed. "I appreciate all you're doing. When are you going to swing by and grab a bite to eat? On the house."

"You don't have to do that," Evelyn said. "I was thinking of coming by with my husband tomorrow night. I can give you an update in person."

"Sounds good," Abigail said. "We do a catfish special on Fridays. I remember you liked our catfish at that lunch we had."

"I love it. And your fried chicken is the best in town."

Abigail chuckled. "That's music to my ears, sugar. See you then."

During her lunch break, Evelyn ate her sandwich then went to the birthing center to visit Megan and Logan. She found mother and child sitting in the rocking chair, the baby sleeping contentedly in Megan's arms.

Evelyn crept closer for a better look, and Megan obligingly turned him slightly so Evelyn could see his tiny face. "Oh, he's adorable."

"Isn't he?" Megan glanced up, waving Anne into the room. "We're holding a meeting of the Logan Brooks fan club."

Anne admired the baby then said, "I have a very important question for you, Megan." After a beat she said, "I need to know what kind of cake you want. For the party." Anne had volunteered to make a cake.

"Party?" Megan sat back, looking surprised. "What party?"

"We're having a Welcome Logan party," Anne said. "Just us, some cake, and a few little gifts."

Megan broke into a huge smile. "Oh, Anne, that is so thoughtful. I was supposed to have a shower in Boston, but it's on hold until I get home. It will be nice to celebrate his birth with you. Thank you."

Anne waved that off. "No problem. We love parties around here, right, Evelyn?"

"We sure do," Evelyn said. "And Anne makes incredible cakes. So pick your flavor."

"I really like chocolate," Megan said. "With vanilla frosting." She wrinkled her nose. "But no blue frosting, even though I had a boy. I don't find it appetizing."

"I won't use it then," Anne said. "How about light green?"

"Much better," Megan said. "I like green, actually. We decorated the nursery in green and white. It's very soothing."

"It sounds pretty," Evelyn said. She wandered over to the bouquets on the windowsill. Megan had three now. Again she did a little grooming so they stayed looking good. "Anne, I got your text. You're going with me to track him down tonight?"

"Wouldn't miss it," Anne said. "Meet me at four, at my car."

Evelyn turned one of the bouquets slightly, placing it to better advantage. Then she walked back over to Megan and the baby.

"What's going on?" Megan asked. "Where are you going?"

"We're gathering information about a hero in the Civil War," Evelyn said, lowering her voice so as not to disturb Logan. "Unfortunately we have to drive out to Colleton County to look at it. Way out in the country."

"But it'll be a nice ride," Anne said. "And an excuse to get out of the city."

"I'd love to see more of South Carolina," Megan commented. "Beyond this hospital room."

"Once Logan is ready to go out, we'll take you two on a walking tour," Anne said. "There's a lot to see right around the hospital."

They chatted about the various sights in Charleston, Megan seeming to be genuinely interested. But Evelyn sensed the tension underlying their casual discussion. How were they ever going to find Harley? Finding one man in a city this size was like looking for a needle in a haystack. But she did have a clue…

"Eep." At the sound, Megan and Anne turned to Evelyn. "Sorry. I just remembered something I forgot to do." She was reluctant to tell Megan and Anne about it until her search bore fruit. It wasn't fair to raise anyone's hopes.

"Hey," Stacia said when Evelyn returned to the office. "How's the baby?" Stacia had heard mention of Megan and Logan, but all she knew was that they were Evelyn's friends. She'd also expressed an interest in helping with Logan's party.

"Great," Evelyn said, stowing her purse. "We talked some more about the party. Anne's making the cake."

"Wonderful. I'll be bringing a veggie platter with dip. That's about the extent of my culinary skills." With a smile, Stacia returned to clacking away on her keyboard.

Evelyn sat at her desk, her phone in hand. An idea was forming in her mind. She opened a map application and searched for A.J.'s Roadhouse. As she'd suspected from the address, it was right off the route they'd be taking to Colleton County tonight. And today was Thursday. "Stacia," she said.

Stacia stopped typing. "Yes, ma'am?"

"You said A.J.'s had good pizza. How are their sandwiches? Anne and I might stop by there tonight, on our way out of town."

Stacia shrugged. "They're good. Regular subs. The burgers and fries are great. Bryce got the platter, and I stole a few of his fries. They were perfect."

Her ill-fated date, the one with the ex-girlfriend who wasn't so ex. "Sorry to remind you about that," Evelyn said. "Thanks."

"There's a menu online, I think," Stacia said.

"I actually have one." Evelyn couldn't hold back a smile. It might be a total wild goose chase, but they had to start somewhere. Hopefully the pizza was good enough to entice an aficionado like Harley Brooks to return.

A.J.'s Roadhouse was a long, low brick building tucked away on a side street. This early in the evening, Anne easily found a space in the parking lot. The only other vehicles there were a few pickup trucks, a motorcycle or two, and several small sedans.

"Ready?" Anne asked, opening the driver's side door.

"Ready," Evelyn echoed. In her phone, she had several new pictures of Harley, sent by Megan. After reflection, she'd realized it probably wasn't the best idea to use the headshot broadcast on the news. Especially if Harley was still operating undercover, which she hoped he was. That was better than the alternative, that he was a criminal on the run.

Inside, the restaurant was dimly lit, the clatter and roll of cue balls drifting from the far end. The walls on each side were lined with booths, tables filled the middle, and a service counter was straight ahead. A young woman sat behind the cash register, a look of boredom on her face.

"Help you?" she asked as they approached. Like the patrons seated here and there, she was casually dressed in T-shirt and jeans, making Evelyn feel even more out of place in her business casual slacks and jacket. But there hadn't been time to run home and change.

"We'd like to place a to-go order," Evelyn said.

The young woman pointed to a stack of printed menus beside the cash register. "Want something to drink while you wait? It'll be about ten to fifteen minutes. Longer if you get pizza."

They weren't ordering pizza tonight, not to eat in the car, so Evelyn said, "Sounds good. I'll take a sweet tea, please."

"Me too," Anne said. "A large. And can we have them in to-go cups? Thanks."

They conferred over the menu while waiting for the server to dispense their tea. "I'm going to have a hot pastrami," Evelyn said, her mouth watering. "Yum." She'd make sure to grab lots of napkins.

"That does sound good," Anne said. "I'll have the same. Want to split an order of fries?"

"Absolutely." Evelyn gave the order to the server and paid in advance. Then she and Anne picked up their cups of tea and moved away from the counter.

"Want to sit?" Anne asked, nodding toward a booth.

That was a tempting idea, but Evelyn knew she couldn't chicken out. "Actually, I want to go check the pool tables." Tonight was Bryce's league night. Hopefully he was here.

"Okay," Anne said, her brows rising. "Lead on."

The pit of Evelyn's stomach tightened as she strolled toward the pool tables, trying to appear relaxed. The truth was, she wasn't a private investigator like the ones she saw on television, cool and savvy and smart. No, she was a middle-aged woman who worked in a hospital.

Several men were clustered around the pool table, two playing and the others looking on. A young man with gelled hair bent over the table and took a shot, banking the cue ball off the side and sending two striped balls into the pocket.

Cheers erupted. "Good one, Bryce," one man said, clapping his friend on the shoulder.

Bryce. That was the name of Stacia's date.

The man Bryce was playing chalked his stick, lips curved in a mock frown. "Yeah, yeah. He got lucky."

Bryce moved back to let the other man take a shot, ending up near Evelyn and Anne. "Hey," he said, throwing a glance over his shoulder. "You ladies here to play pool?" There were two other tables, both empty. "The rest of the league isn't here yet, so go ahead."

"No, we're waiting on a to-go order," Evelyn said. She took a deep breath, inadvertently inhaling Bryce's strong aftershave. "Do you know Stacia Westbrook? She mentioned this place to me." *And you.* "We work together at Mercy Hospital."

His eyes lit up. "Yeah. Stacia. So you work with her?"

"Bryce," his pool rival called. "Your turn."

"Excuse me," Bryce said. "Be right back." He strode to the table and made another great shot that cleared the eight ball. Game over.

"You won, buddy," his rival said. "But I'll get you next time."

Bryce shrugged that off with a laugh as he returned to Evelyn and Anne. "So how's Stacia doing?"

"She's great," Evelyn said. The vise in her belly tightened a notch. It was now or never. "You spend a lot of time here?"

Bryce twirled his pool cue. "My buddies and I stop by here a few times a week. Play a couple of games, get something to eat. Tonight we have our pool league."

"You work nearby?" Anne asked. She smiled. "I'm Anne and this is Evelyn."

He nodded. "Bryce." His face screwed up at his blunder. "But you already know that. Yeah, we work at a warehouse nearby, so this is convenient, you might say."

It was nice for young men to have a place to gather. And it also meant they were here on a regular basis. Evelyn pulled out her phone. "Bryce, I have something to ask you." She brought up a picture of Harley, a nice shot of him outside, wind in his hair and with a big smile. "Have you seen this man?"

Bryce looked taken aback, but he accepted the phone. "Why are you looking for him?"

What to say? Evelyn glanced at Anne, drawing strength from her friend's encouraging expression. "His family is looking for him. He moved down here and dropped out of sight." Sensing his hesitation, she added, "They want to know he's all right."

"Okay." Bryce drew the word out. He stabbed at the phone screen with a forefinger before handing it back. "And yeah, that's Lee."

Chapter Fifteen

Satisfaction surged through Evelyn. They'd found Harley Brooks, the needle in the haystack. Evelyn marveled at how the pieces had come together, a sure sign of God's hand in the situation. Hearing about Stacia's date, finding the menu, Bryce being here tonight...it was all too wonderful. And Harley calling himself Lee? That was clever. She wished she could ask for the last name he was using, but she didn't dare.

"I don't know where he's living or anything, but he's been hanging around with the daily workers," Bryce went on. "You know, the guys who try to get picked for extra jobs in the warehouses or unloading ships."

Evelyn had heard about day laborers, who worked on a temporary basis. What a smart way for Harley to infiltrate businesses. "So he seems like he's doing okay?" she asked.

"Yeah, as far as I know," Bryce said. "He comes in here now and then and plays pool." His lips curved in a wry smile. "He even beat me a couple of times."

"Evelyn?" the server called at the other end of the room. "Order's up."

"That's my cue," Evelyn said. "Thanks, Bryce. Have a good night."

Evelyn practically racewalked through the restaurant, her veins bubbling with relief and joy. They'd made big progress tonight.

"He's using the name Lee?" Anne asked as she unlocked the car a couple of minutes later. "That's pretty clever."

"That's what I thought." Evelyn climbed into the passenger seat and set her drink in the cup holder. "It's another thing that proves it's really him." The aroma rising from the hot sandwiches was making her mouth water.

Anne did the same with her iced tea and started the car. "Now we need to find out where he's staying. And where he works."

"I think we will." Evelyn's heart lifted in confidence. She pulled napkins from the bag, trying to figure out how they could eat without making a mess. "I can't wait to tell Megan." She thought about sending a text but decided against it. News like this was too important to share on the phone.

Anne had backed and turned the car, ready to enter the street. "Come on, come on," she said, waiting for an SUV to go past. Finally it did and she pulled out. "On to the Combahee Heritage Society."

They were soon on the main route, passing through commercial areas that gradually dwindled into long stretches of land between sporadic settlements. The sun was setting in front of them, sinking into a red band of clouds across the horizon.

"It gets dark so early," Evelyn commented. "I hate the short days this time of year." And it would be another month before they started lengthening again.

"Me too," Anne said. "The flip side is, they give us a good excuse to get cozy at home in the evening."

"I don't mind that," Evelyn said, thinking of her quiet evenings with James. They might not talk much sometimes, but it was comforting being with him in the same room. She sent him a text to check in and let him know where they were.

As they left the city behind, traffic had thinned, and there were very few cars on the road in either direction. But they had barely crossed the Colleton County line when bright headlights came behind them, much too fast. By the height of the lights, the vehicle appeared to be a pickup truck or large SUV.

Anne adjusted her mirror, squinting. "That's annoying. Why doesn't he go around?" Both sides of this highway were double lanes, which meant legal passing at any point. But the driver remained behind the car, shadowing them.

"Try slowing down," Evelyn said. "Then they'll pass us."

But when Anne hit the brakes, the other vehicle did as well, staying a certain distance behind them. With a sigh, Anne sped up, back to the speed limit. "We're almost there. I guess I can put up with it."

The tailgater remained with them until they reached Jacksonboro. Evelyn read off directions to Anne and soon they were turning down a side street. Glancing back over her shoulder, Evelyn saw the vehicle roar by, able only to identify it as a dark SUV.

"He's gone, thank goodness," she said. "The heritage society should be coming right up on your left."

The Combahee River Heritage Society was located in a historic cottage with a wide L-shaped porch. Cheerful lights shone through tall front windows, indicating that the place was open, as promised.

The entrance door led directly into a wide foyer, where a middle-aged woman with gray-sprinkled curly hair sat working on a computer. When she saw Anne and Evelyn, she rose heavily to her feet, flicking the cardigan around her shoulders into place. "Good evening," she said, her voice low and resonant. "How can I help you?"

Evelyn stepped forward. "Patricia Cooper from the Charleston Heritage Society recommended I come over. I'm looking for the Benjamin Gibbs plantation records."

"Oh, Patricia," the woman said. "She's a good friend of mine." She gestured. "Come right this way. I'm Myra."

The women followed, introducing themselves. Myra led them through a long room with two fireplaces, obviously once a double living room. But now it held display cases, bookcases, and antique tools and the like.

A portrait on one wall caught Evelyn's eye. "That's Belinda Gibbs," she said, recognizing Mary Lou's ancestor. In this painting, she was seated on a sofa with her arms around two children. A man stood behind her, along with two older children.

Myra halted. "It is, yes. With her husband Benjamin and their family. They had one of the largest rice plantations on the Combahee." She continued walking, leading them into a smaller room where a microfilm reader was set up on a desk. "Have a seat, and I'll get the roll. Which dates do you want?"

"How about 1860 to 1863?" Evelyn said. That would cut down the documents they had to wade through.

"Go ahead," Anne said, indicating the desk chair. She pulled another chair close. "I'll look on."

As they got settled, Myra rummaged through the file cabinet. "Here we go." She brought the roll over and showed Evelyn how to thread it through the roller. "You can control the speed," she said, "and I recommend going slowly. Scrolling too fast will make you dizzy."

"Oh, I know," Evelyn said. She turned on the machine then flipped through blank pages until the first document came on the screen.

Myra handed Anne a binder. "This has an index to the roll. See?" She flipped it open to the right page. "You can print any screens you want and then pay at the desk. Ten cents a page."

"Thanks," Anne said, placing the open binder on the desk.

"I'll leave you to it," Myra said, moving toward the door. "Holler if you need anything."

Evelyn turned to Anne. "So what do we have?" Together they studied the page.

"The expense ledger for freedmen sounds right," Anne said. "We should look for the latest entry that mentions Israel working for Gibbs as a river pilot."

"Good call, Anne. That would mean he was still visiting the plantations." With a few rolls of the tape, Evelyn found the right ledger. She zoomed in on the image so they could read the cramped entries on yellowed pages.

They flipped through the book, pausing whenever they spotted Israel's name. He appeared to be paid sporadically, probably whenever he piloted one of the plantation's boats down the river and back.

"Here we go," Evelyn said. "A payment to Israel at the end of May 1863."

"The raid was the following week, right?" Anne asked. "So he was still working as a river pilot. And going to the Gibbs Plantation, which was raided. We've verified that much at least."

"That's what Sabra's account says," Evelyn noted. "So far it seems to be accurate."

Myra popped back into the room. "Sorry to interrupt, but I have a question." Once they were both looking at her, she said, "We have a lot of resources here regarding the Gibbs family. Is there anything in particular I can help you with?"

"Actually," Evelyn explained, "we're interested in a man who worked for the Gibbs family. Israel Gibbs was his name, and he was a river pilot."

Anne took up the tale. "A museum in Charleston is doing a special exhibit about the Combahee River Raid, and a descendant of his wants him to be included."

"So we're looking for sources that prove he was there," Evelyn concluded. She pointed at the screen. "We just found proof that he was working as a river pilot right before the raid."

"Israel Gibbs, huh?" Myra's brow furrowed. "Where have I seen that name?"

Evelyn didn't prompt the historian, giving her space to remember. After a moment, Myra held up a finger, practically trotting over to a bookcase. Bending down, she eased a scrapbook out from between other volumes.

She carried the book to a nearby table and opened it then began to leaf through. Evelyn and Anne joined her, standing on either side.

"This scrapbook has a lot of information about the Gibbs family," Myra said. "We made them for all the prominent families."

Over her shoulder, Evelyn viewed the pages, which held newspaper articles, photographs, copies of deeds, and other ephemera.

"Here we go." Myra tapped the page beside what appeared to be a letter. "This is from a Union general who wrote to support Harriet Tubman's pension claim. He lists the names of the river pilots and scouts who helped her the night of the raid."

Evelyn bent closer, wishing the letter had been typed. It was written in swirling penmanship like so many documents from the era. But once she could translate the script, she clearly saw the name Israel Gibbs.

"This is so exciting," Anne said. "Now we have actual proof that Israel Gibbs was there."

"He never got a military pension, so that was a dead end," Evelyn said. "I was starting to think that we wouldn't find anything."

"We're hoping to host that exhibit this summer," Myra said. "Cora Beth promised to send it on the road, so to speak."

"What a great idea," Evelyn said. "I'm sure people in this area would love to see it. It fits in with your overall work." She pulled out her phone. "Do you mind if I take a picture of this? I want to show it to Cora Beth."

Myra stepped back. "Go right ahead. This is only a photocopy. The real document is in an archives in Washington, DC, I believe."

Evelyn snapped a picture and made sure it was clear. "We're going to poke around a little more," she said, thinking they might as well take advantage while they were there. "We have time, right?"

"Another hour until we close," Myra said. "So please, research to your heart's content." Once again, she headed out into the other room.

Anne turned the page in the scrapbook. "I wonder if there's anything else about Israel in here."

The first couple of pages held articles about the raid, clipped from various newspapers. "These are the same sources Cora Beth used," Evelyn said, recognizing the publications.

She studied the articles carefully, but Israel's name wasn't mentioned. Not that it surprised her, since Cora Beth hadn't seen him included either, hence the reluctance to list him as one of Harriet's scouts. Maybe Evelyn could get over to the library archives tomorrow and widen her search into these particular newspapers.

"All set?" At Evelyn's nod, Anne turned the page. "What's this?"

PLANTATION OWNER SHOT IN COLD BLOOD, screamed a headline from September 1863.

Evelyn bent closer, scanning the article hastily. "It says that Benjamin Gibbs was shot at his house in Charleston after accosting a man who was breaking in. The man pulled a revolver and fired twice, striking Mr. Gibbs and killing him instantly."

"Wow, that's tragic," Anne said.

"'The intruder got away, Belinda Gibbs said,'" Evelyn read. But when she took in the next sentence, her throat dried up. No. It couldn't be true.

"What is it?" Anne asked. "Are you okay?"

"I'm fine," Evelyn said, a hand to her throat. "But in shock. Listen to this." She swallowed and then read, "'Mrs. Gibbs claimed that the man who had so rudely tried to illicitly enter her home was a former employee, a man by the name of Israel Gibbs.'"

Chapter Sixteen

"No way," Anne exclaimed. "I don't believe it." She nudged Evelyn with her shoulder, trying to get a better look. "Are you sure it says Israel Gibbs?"

"Positive," Evelyn said, moving the book so Anne could see it better. "Read it for yourself."

Anne read the article, her lips pursed. "I still don't believe it. Why would Israel Gibbs try to rob a house, especially that one? Why would he go anywhere near Benjamin Gibbs after the raid on the Gibbs plantation?"

"I agree, it doesn't make sense," Evelyn said. "I'm sure Israel and the others who helped Harriet laid low for a while. They had to know they would be regarded as traitors."

Anne thought for a moment. "Remember how Shirley said Israel was considered a scoundrel? Is this why?"

Evelyn flipped through the book but there were no more articles about the murder or its aftermath. "Must be. And if he's guilty, then I get why they'd say that."

"But you doubt it," Anne said.

"Yes, I do." Evelyn's shock was receding, and her mind was kicking into gear again. "He had helped free the people he cared about and many more, so he'd won. Why would he feel he needed to seek further revenge?" She flipped back to the article reporting Benjamin's murder. "According to this, Belinda Gibbs was a witness. But what if she was wrong?"

"Maybe she only thought it was Israel," Anne said. "It happened at night, right?"

Evelyn thought of something else. "If Israel was arrested, why didn't they hang him? That was the penalty for murder back then, wasn't it?"

"I believe so," Anne said. "But he was obviously alive long enough to tell Sabra his story."

"She wrote it in 1905, the year Abigail said he died, and the way it's worded, it sounds like he dictated it to her," Evelyn said. "She was only a baby when the raid happened and when Benjamin was shot."

"If only he'd talked about Benjamin's murder," Anne said. "Then it wouldn't be such a mystery."

"I know, right?" Evelyn's spirits sank. How was she going to bring this topic up to Abigail? Did she have to? But if Cora Beth got wind of it—or already knew—she'd probably not want to include an accused killer in the exhibit. Maybe that had been the reason for her reluctance all along.

"Let me look one more time." Anne leafed through the scrapbook again. "What a shame. There's nothing else about the murder."

"Go back to the first article," Evelyn said. She used her phone to take a couple of snapshots to study later. "I wonder if Myra knows anything about this."

"I'll go ask." Anne slipped out of the room.

She returned a moment later with Myra. "As Anne probably mentioned, we found this article about Benjamin Gibbs being murdered during a burglary," Evelyn said. "Do you know anything about what happened? Or do you have other sources that talk about it?"

Myra came closer, a curious expression on her face as she bent to scan the headline. "I know about his murder. But that's all. Life was pretty chaotic during the war, you understand. Charleston was bombed almost continuously. Lots of crazy things happened."

"So you've never done an exhibit featuring Benjamin's untimely death?" Evelyn asked, already guessing the answer.

"Oh no," Myra said. "It happened in Charleston. We focus on the history of this area. We have our hands full with everything that happened around here."

Evelyn supposed that one murder in the shadow of two hundred years of history and the Civil War would be a pretty minor item. Although Benjamin's death certainly hadn't been minor for the poor Gibbs family. What a horrible thing for his wife to witness. Evelyn felt great compassion for the woman despite what she believed was Belinda's mistaken identification of the killer.

"Is there anything else I can do for you?" Myra asked.

Anne glanced at Evelyn, who shook her head. "No, I think we're all set. Thank you for your help."

"Yes, thank you, Myra," Evelyn said. "I can't wait to share the general's letter with Israel's family. Abigail is going to be thrilled."

After Myra left the room, Anne said, "What are we going to do now?"

Evelyn closed the scrapbook. "We're going to figure out the rest of the story. Israel was a hero, and he deserves that much."

Evelyn was on her way to visit Megan when she spotted a familiar figure walking ahead. "Hey, Shirley," she called. "Wait up."

The nurse halted, turning around with a shake of her braid. "Hey, Evelyn. How are you this morning?"

"A little tired but great overall." Evelyn hurried to reach her friend. "Anne and I had a very productive outing last night." She couldn't wait to tell Megan that Harley had been spotted at A.J.'s Roadhouse. But talking to Abigail about the accusation of murder against Israel? Not so much. Evelyn hoped she could figure out something before she saw Abigail later.

As they fell into step, Shirley said, "I take it you're talking about Megan's husband."

"I am," Evelyn said. Speaking in low tones, she told Shirley that Harley was still in Charleston, using another alias. "He's been working in the warehouses near the docks, according to a young man Stacia knows."

"Sounds to me like he's still on his mission," Shirley said. "Things fell apart at the bank, so he's coming at it from another angle."

"You could be right," Evelyn said. "At least we know he didn't skip out of the country."

They had reached their destination, and after speaking to the guard, they went through the locked door into the birthing center. At this time of day, the unit was fairly quiet as mothers and babies enjoyed breakfast and medical personnel updated charts.

Megan looked up with a smile when they knocked. "Good morning," she said, her hand on the bassinet holding her sleeping son.

Evelyn and Shirley tiptoed forward to peek at the baby. "He gets cuter every day," Evelyn said. "And bigger."

Megan smiled at Logan. "He's doing well, they said. He'll probably be here a couple more weeks though."

Shirley picked up one of the flower vases. "You talk to Evelyn while I tidy up a bit. This one needs more water." She carried the vase to the bathroom and turned on the faucet.

"Is there any news?" Megan's eyes were huge in her pale face. Her fingers tightened on the edge of the bassinet.

Evelyn nodded, unable to hold back a grin. "I didn't want to say anything until we were sure, but I think we've tracked Harley down." She put up a hand when Megan gasped. "We don't know where he's living—yet—but he's hanging around down by the docks. Under a false identity, of course. A friend of a friend identified him by his picture." A friend of a friend was the best way to label Bryce, she decided. The real story was too complicated.

Megan understood immediately. "He's still on the job." Her eyes widened again but this time with confusion. "But why didn't Carson tell me that? Instead he keeps saying that Harley went rogue and ran off with the bank's money."

"I know, I've heard him," Evelyn said. Carson's actions were a mystery to her at this point. She also wasn't sure what they should do next to find Harley. The words *trust and obey* floated into her mind. Good advice. So far, clues were being revealed gradually. "Take one step at a time, Megan, and have faith. That's all we can do. We're getting there."

Shirley carried the flowers back into the room and set them on the sill, then checked the other vases. Apparently deciding they were fine, she came over to the bassinet. "Did you and Anne have any luck last night in Colleton County?"

"Yes and no," Evelyn said. "We found official proof that Israel Gibbs was involved in the raid, hurray. But then we discovered something that's really troubling." Evelyn handed Shirley her phone, open to her photo library.

"Excellent," Shirley said, reading the general's letter. "Good work, Evelyn." She showed the phone to Megan, pointing at Israel's name. "He's a real hero, and this proves it."

"Now go to the next image," Evelyn said.

Shirley swiped, as directed, and scanned the short article. "Oh my. I never knew the details, why they called him a scoundrel. This is serious business."

"You've got that right," Evelyn said. "But there has to be more to the story. I'm going to continue looking until I find it."

Megan smiled at Shirley. "Isn't she a wonder?"

"She's got a gift, all right," Shirley said. "I'm grateful to have her on my team."

The young mother turned to Evelyn. "I love your determination too. It's really encouraging me to stay strong." She threw her arms around Evelyn. "You're the best."

Pleased, flattered, and humbled, Evelyn felt her cheeks burn. She gave Megan a squeeze in return. "I don't know about that. But I try to do what I can."

"That's all the good Lord asks of us," Shirley said. She peeked into the bassinet. "It looks like our young sir is about to wake up."

She reached out and touched Logan with a gentle hand. "Aren't you handsome? I bet your daddy's going to be real proud of you."

In response, the baby blinked his eyes and cooed, a sweet sound that made them all sigh. Megan gathered him into her arms. "Say hello to Mommy's friends, Logan."

"Here you go." Evelyn set a tall to-go coffee on Stacia's desk. She'd swung by the cafeteria after leaving the birthing center.

"Thanks, Evelyn," Stacia said, picking up the cup. "How did you know I was going to run out for coffee in a minute?"

"I didn't," Evelyn said with a laugh. "But you always go for me, so I thought I'd return the favor." She set her cup on the desk and placed her handbag on the floor.

Stacia took a sip of coffee then swiveled her chair back and forth, grinning. "Notice anything different?"

Evelyn's gaze swept her assistant from head to toe, looking for a new haircut or outfit. "No, not really. You look great as always."

"Gee, thanks, Evelyn. That's nice to hear." Stacia pointed to the back of the room. "But I'm not talking about me."

Evelyn turned and looked. For a moment or two, she didn't realize what she was looking at. Then it sank in. The stepladders were gone. The ceiling tiles were back in place, some of them brand new. And most telling of all, the door to the Vault was opened a crack. Stacia must have unlocked it.

"They're all done?" Evelyn took a step forward. "I thought it was going to be off-limits until Monday."

"It was," Stacia said. "But Cliff told me this morning they got everything buttoned up faster than he thought."

"I can't believe it." Evelyn walked across the floor to the Vault, where she pushed the door open wide. "I've missed this place so much." She flicked on the light switch, revealing the familiar shelves, cupboards, and cabinets, all stuffed with historical records and artifacts. The repository of Mercy Hospital's long and storied history.

Would she find anything mentioning Israel Gibbs inside? She couldn't wait to find out.

Chapter Seventeen

AFTER RETURNING TO HER DESK, Evelyn looked up the library archive hours on her phone. Her plan was to take a bus to the branch at lunch and research the murder of Benjamin Gibbs. Walking there would take over twenty minutes, which wouldn't give her much time at the library. If she worked late tonight, she could also take a longer lunch hour, which she did now and then.

"Mind if I change my lunch hour a little?" Evelyn asked Stacia. "I need to take a bus to the library." She gave Stacia the times she expected to leave and return.

"No problemo," Stacia said. "I brought lunch. Leftover pizza."

"That sounds good." The mention of pizza reminded Evelyn of Bryce. "Guess who I met last night? Bryce."

Stacia rocked back in her chair. "Really? What did you think?"

"He's a good-looking guy, you have to give him that," Evelyn said. "He seemed nice enough."

Stacia pushed out her lower lip. "How did you happen to talk to him?"

"Anne and I stopped by A.J.'s for sandwiches," Evelyn said. "While we were waiting for our order, we checked out the pool tables. He was playing a game, and I heard someone say his name." Evelyn guessed what Stacia was wondering. "I asked him if he knew you. Said I worked with you. But I didn't mention your date, of course."

"What did he say?" Stacia's eyes gleamed with interest.

"Oh, his face lit right up. He asked how you were doing."

Stacia stared into space, considering this. Then a sly smile crept across her face. "Maybe he regrets what he did. Dumping me on our date to talk to his ex, I mean."

"I'm sure he does," Evelyn said. "The grass is always greener…"

Stacia laughed. "It sounds like a soap opera, doesn't it?" She stretched with a smile. "I have to admit it feels good to hear that. But, once burned…"

"Don't blame you a bit." Evelyn's computer pinged as emails popped into her in-box. "And I'd better get to work." She glanced at Stacia, who was already on her computer again. "By the way, you were right. The food at A.J.'s is great."

Stacia nodded. "Sure is. Maybe we can go there for pizza sometime."

"Sounds good." Evelyn's phone rang, and she grabbed it. "Good morning. This is Evelyn Perry in the Records Department. How may I help you?"

The library was modern, spacious, and hushed, a book lover's delight. After getting directions from the front desk, Evelyn made her way to the archives room. Here she asked a librarian named Nancy about viewing newspapers from the nineteenth century. "I'm looking for Charleston newspapers from 1863 and after," she explained.

"About any topic in particular?" Nancy asked, adjusting her cat-eye glasses. The librarian, who had short, coiffed blond hair and impeccable makeup, wore a cardigan around her shoulders like Myra had. For a surreal moment Evelyn wondered if it was some kind of archival uniform.

"I'm researching the Combahee River Raid in June 1863." Evelyn hesitated, wondering if she should mention her real reason for coming here. "And the murder of Benjamin Gibbs in September 1863."

Nancy tilted her head. "Oh, are you a true crime aficionado? We get quite a few people in here researching Charleston's unsolved mysteries."

Evelyn's heart gave a thump. "Was Benjamin's murder unsolved?"

"I don't know all the details," Nancy said. "My area of expertise is genealogy. But I can point you in the right direction."

"I'd appreciate that," Evelyn said.

The librarian came around the end of the counter. "Let me show you how to get into the system." She escorted Evelyn to a computer station nearby and brought the screen back to life. "This is the database for the newspaper articles. You can search by keyword."

"That's great," Evelyn said. She'd pictured herself having to leaf through back issues trying to find relevant articles. Nancy moved aside, and she sat at the station. "Can I print?"

"You can, for a nominal fee," Nancy said. "You can also email the results to yourself."

"Wonderful." Maybe she should do both, print a copy and store the article in her email as well. She pulled out her notebook and pen so she could also jot notes.

"I'll be at the desk if you need me," Nancy said.

"Thanks, Nancy," Evelyn said. She poised her fingers over the keyboard, staring at the blinking cursor beside the search box. Then she typed in, ISRAEL GIBBS.

No results.

Evelyn held back a grunt of frustration. Maybe she would have to resort to a page-by-page search. Then she thought about the researchers who had indexed the articles. They'd had to do their best to make an index useful, but including every event and person would make it incredibly unwieldy.

She typed in, BENJAMIN GIBBS.

Yes, success. A list of links filled the page. Ignoring the ones before the murder, Evelyn clicked on a link. This was the same article she'd read at the heritage society the previous evening.

She went to the next article, which said, "SUSPECT IN CITY SLAYING GOES MISSING."

After giving a brief description of events—an intruder seeking to rob the Gibbs residence shot the householder, Benjamin Gibbs, in the entrance hall—it went on to say, *"Police have been unable to locate one Israel Gibbs of Charleston. Formerly employed by the late Mr. Gibbs as a river pilot, Israel Gibbs was identified at the scene by an eyewitness."*

Evelyn's heart sank and she may even have groaned. If someone saw Israel shoot Benjamin, then that was a pretty open-and-shut case.

After sending the article to print and to her email, Evelyn glanced at the other articles but didn't find any updates on the case. One detailed Benjamin's funeral but only said that the "guilty party is still on the loose."

She began to skim through the issues but didn't find any other articles about the case. It wasn't entirely surprising since the state was in the thick of a war. And on top of that, an epidemic of yellow fever struck later in the fall.

Difficult times in Charleston, for sure.

Evelyn logged out of the database and gathered her things. She needed to catch the bus and return to work. Hopefully by the time she saw Abigail tonight, she'd figure how to frame what she'd learned.

James drove them over to Abigail's Kitchen, which was located on a street near Mother Emmanuel Church. The former boardinghouse and longtime restaurant was housed in a two-story frame building painted a cheerful red.

"Here we are," James said as he parallel parked a short distance down the block. He came around to help Evelyn out of the car, keeping his arm around her as they strolled down the sidewalk.

"I still don't know what to tell her," Evelyn said. She'd confided everything to James that afternoon, after he'd gotten out of work.

"How about leading with the good news?" James said. He'd already made this suggestion, but his tone was as patient as ever.

They reached the restaurant entrance, and James opened the door for Evelyn. Bells jingled as she walked into the steamy, delicious-smelling space that was Abigail's Kitchen. Straight ahead was a counter, with several people working behind the line, and to each side and along the front wall were booths and a few tables. The day's menu was on the board hanging over the counter. Most of the tables were filled, and there was a short line waiting to order. Silverware and dishes clattered, and voices murmured and laughed.

"I want a booth," Evelyn said, spotting an empty one with a view of the street. She went in that direction, taking off her jacket. She placed it on the seat to hold it. James did the same on the bench opposite.

Together they got in line. Evelyn studied the menu while they waited, although she already knew what she wanted. Catfish, mac and cheese, and sweet potatoes.

"Can I take your order?" a young man asked when they reached the head of the line. He was trim and attractive, wearing a spotless white apron and cap.

They placed their orders then Evelyn asked, "Is Abigail here tonight?"

The server glanced over his shoulder. "Yes, she is. Working in back."

"Can you please tell her that Evelyn Perry is here? I'd love to talk to her if she has a moment."

"Will do, ma'am." He accepted a card from James and ran it through. "Get your drinks over there, and we'll call you when your order is up."

They moved along to the drinks counter, where they dispensed ice and sweet tea into cups. On the way to their booth, Evelyn took a sip, enjoying the cool sweetness flooding her mouth. Even the tea was extra good here at Abigail's.

While waiting for their food, Evelyn and James drank tea and people watched, content to sit together in silence. Evelyn allowed her busy mind to pause and enjoy the moment, trusting her conversation with Abigail would go all right.

"James," bellowed a large, handsome man behind the line.

With a smile, James slid out of the booth. "Be right back." He went up to the counter, where he took possession of a tray and added napkin-wrapped silverware.

"Wow," Evelyn said, sitting back as he placed a loaded plate in front of her. "I hope I can eat all this."

"We can get to-go boxes," James said, taking his seat again. "Although that won't be a problem for me." He picked up a bottle of hot sauce and sprinkled it on his fish.

Evelyn took her first bite of catfish, tender under a crunchy coating. "Yum. This is so good."

They were almost finished when Abigail came out front and headed over to their table. "Hey, Evelyn. Marvin told me you were here." Anxiety flickered in her big brown eyes. "Do you have any news for me?"

"Have a seat," James said. He slid his plate across the table and then came over to Evelyn's side.

Abigail did as he suggested, reaching out her hand with a smile. "You must be Evelyn's husband. I think I've seen you in here before."

"Oh you have," James said, shaking her hand before sitting down. "I'm James. Nice to officially meet you."

"Likewise," Abigail said. She rested her elbows on the table. "How was everything?"

"Absolutely delicious," Evelyn said, putting her fork down. Despite her earlier protests, she'd decimated almost everything on her plate, as her tight waistband now testified.

"That's what we like to hear," Abigail said. "The catfish is an old recipe from the original Abigail."

"She certainly was a gifted cook," James said. "Southern food at its best."

Evelyn gathered her thoughts then began. "Since we last spoke, I found the proof you need about Israel."

Abigail jumped in her seat, giving a cry of "Hallelujah" that drew the attention of the whole restaurant.

Evelyn picked up her phone and scrolled to the general's letter. "He was mentioned specifically in this letter regarding Harriet Tubman's mission." She passed the phone over so Abigail could see it.

"Can you send that to me?" Abigail's grin was luminous. "I think the word of a general should be good enough, right?"

"I agree," Evelyn said. She dug in her handbag and pulled out several pages. "We also looked at the Gibbs Plantation ledger and found that Israel was working as a river pilot at the time."

Abigail took the pages. "This is really thorough. Cora Beth isn't going to be able to say no now, is she?" she crowed.

"I don't think she can," Evelyn said. "And I hope to find more about his actual work during the raid. That will round out his story."

"It sure will." Abigail placed the pages on the table. "Is there anything else?"

Evelyn glanced at James, who gave her a subtle nod. "There is. And quite frankly, it's confusing me."

A troubled expression creased Abigail's brow. "What do you mean?" Her tone was wary.

Evelyn took out the articles related to the murder. "Before I give these to you, I want to say this. I think Israel was innocent." She slid the pages to Abigail.

Abigail studied the pages briefly before tossing them aside with a frown. "What does that mess have to do with his heroism?"

"Nothing," Evelyn admitted. "But I'm thinking we should be prepared to address it. What if someone comes forward and objects to his inclusion in the exhibit?"

"Do you really think they would?" Then Abigail barked a laugh. "Of course they would. This is Charleston, where history never dies. And neither do old scandals."

"Exactly." The knot in Evelyn's belly uncoiled a little. She'd survived the first hurdle. Abigail hadn't yelled at her or thrown her out of the restaurant. "What do you know about this, Abigail? Obviously—"

She was interrupted by the large, handsome man, who arrived at the table, bowls of banana pudding in his hands. "Thanks, Tito," Abigail said as he set them in front of Evelyn and James. "On the house."

"Oh, I love your banana pudding." Evelyn picked up the spoon and swirled it through the whipped cream on top.

"I'm glad," Abigail said. Placing a hand on the man's arm, she said, "This is my husband, Tito. Tito, these are friends of mine. James and Evelyn."

"Nice to meet you both," Tito said, his voice a velvet grumble.

Evelyn and James said hello. "We love eating here," Evelyn said, echoed by James.

"That's what we like to hear," Tito said. After bestowing a wide, welcoming smile, he turned and hurried back across the restaurant.

"As you were saying?" Abigail returned to the topic of Israel.

Evelyn took a taste of whipped cream then reluctantly put the spoon down. "I was about to say that obviously Israel was cleared somehow. He lived a good, long life, and he didn't spend it in jail."

"No, he didn't. He lived right here"—she pointed to the ceiling—"in this house, until he went into the hospital with his final illness and died at age sixty-five. Not a long life by today's standards but for those days, yes, a decent span." She paused then said, "I never knew exactly what went on, only that he'd gotten in some kind of trouble. But our focus was always on his brave service to our country."

"As it should be," James put in. He'd been silent so far, listening to the conversation. "Evelyn, you didn't find any articles about his trial or acquittal, did you?"

"No, I didn't," Evelyn said. "I thought maybe it was because they were in the middle of a war. And a yellow fever outbreak."

"Still," James said, "a high profile murder like Benjamin's should have warranted some coverage. Especially if they thought he was killed by a former employee."

"Revenge, you mean?" Abigail said. "Yes, I'm sure they were worried about that. But to me, the best revenge Israel could have had was setting those captives free. The plantations couldn't operate without them."

"Very true," James said. "Freedom was a death blow to that way of life."

Abigail's point was valid, Evelyn thought, but it only proved how strange it was that Israel hadn't gone to prison or been hanged. "He must have been caught and cleared somehow. Maybe he had an alibi."

"Maybe," Abigail said. "Though I'm not sure they would have listened to him over the word of Mrs. Gibbs. Especially after he helped with the raid. Let me take a look through the family papers. Sabra kept a journal but, sad to say, I haven't read it all. Maybe there's something in there that talks about all this."

"Could you do that?" Evelyn asked eagerly. "Or if you don't have time to read it right now, I can take a peek. Unless you'd rather I didn't." Some people were funny about having outsiders read family papers. "I'll take good care of it, I promise."

"Why not?" Abigail said. "Seems like you know all our secrets already. I'll dig it out and give you a call tomorrow, how's that?" The grin was back. "And maybe you can come with me to talk to Cora Beth tomorrow evening, show her the general's letter."

"I'd be happy to," Evelyn said. She picked up her spoon and scooped up a mouthful of banana pudding. She'd made it through a difficult conversation, and this delicious dessert was the perfect reward.

Full darkness had fallen by the time Evelyn and James left the restaurant.

"I can't wait to read Sabra's journal," she said to James as they strolled arm in arm along the sidewalk to the car. "I'm sure it will be fascinating." She especially hoped that Sabra had written about the murder and its aftermath.

James chuckled. "We're a couple of history nerds, aren't we?"

But instead of answering, Evelyn's attention was caught by a vehicle slowly rolling down the street, matching their pace. A large, dark SUV. Exactly like the one she'd seen near A.J.'s.

Chapter Eighteen

Evelyn tugged on her husband's arm, making him stop walking. "James. I think that SUV is following us."

James glanced at the vehicle, which was still moving at a snail's pace. "They're probably looking for a place to park." He began moving again. "Why would you think they're interested in us?"

"Because I saw an SUV exactly like that yesterday, outside the restaurant Anne and I stopped at. And I think he followed us to Colleton County. Someone was tailing us a good portion of the way."

James threw her a sharp glance. "You didn't say anything about that last night." Despite his doubt about the vehicle's intent, he had pulled out the car keys, Evelyn noticed.

"Because I thought maybe I was imagining it." Evelyn kept her gaze on the SUV, trying to read the license plate. But one of the plate lights was out. The driver sped up, and soon the SUV reached the end of the block, signaled a turn, and then vanished into the night. Phew. "And maybe I am again. He's gone."

James aimed the fob and unlocked the car. "It's good to be cautious, and I'm glad you are." He opened the passenger door for Evelyn. "Please, tell me if you see anything or anyone suspicious. Promise?"

Evelyn looked up at James, and even in the dim glow from a nearby streetlight, she could see the worry in his eyes. What a good husband he was. "Promise."

The next day was Saturday, so Evelyn slept in, just a little past her usual rising time. Then she enjoyed a leisurely breakfast with James on their balcony, because it was such a warm day. They had scrambled eggs, bacon, and cranberry muffins from a local bakery.

Evelyn turned her face to the sun with a sigh. "Oh, this feels so good."

"Better enjoy it," James said. He was reading the news on his tablet. "According to the weather report, we're getting a cold snap tonight."

"I don't mind too much," Evelyn said. "This time of year we're meant to get cozy indoors." She thought about the old-fashioned oyster and cracker dressing she wanted to try. "I'm roasting a turkey breast tomorrow for Sunday dinner. A little foretaste of Thanksgiving." Plus she would slice up the meat for sandwiches and turkey potpie.

James read her mind. "Testing out another dressing on me?"

Evelyn hid her smile. "I am." She didn't mention the ingredients, preferring to surprise him. "What are you up to today?"

"Not much," James said. "Puttering around here this morning, a round of golf this afternoon. How about you?"

"I'm thinking about going over to the hospital to see Megan. I want to talk to her about the Welcome Logan party, plus, to be honest, I'm keeping an eye on her." Evelyn's heart ached whenever she considered the young mother's situation. "The longer her husband is missing, the harder it is for her to stay hopeful and positive."

"I'll bet," James said. "I haven't seen anything more on the news about Harley. Or should I say David Smith. Or his whereabouts."

"But he's still around. I'm so glad we found Bryce to confirm it." Evelyn had already told James about her conversation with Stacia's date, after her return from Colleton County.

"Do you think you should go to the police with that information?" James asked.

"No." Evelyn's answer was vehement. "Not yet, anyway. I don't believe he's guilty of anything. If he was, he'd be long gone, in the Caribbean or something." She shivered. "Revealing where he is might lead to him getting killed. I don't want that on my conscience."

James put up a hand. "Hold on, Evelyn. It was only a question. It's not like you saw him in person or anything. Maybe Bryce was wrong."

Evelyn doubted it but said, "Could be. All I know is, I'm praying for Megan and her sweet little baby, that her family will be reunited and safe."

"Me too," James said. "My heart goes out to her. It really does."

"And I love that about you," Evelyn said. She drank the last sip of coffee. "I'm going in for a refill if you want one."

Since it was Saturday, Evelyn wore jeans, a blouse, and leather booties to the hospital. But despite her casual attire, she sported a special brooch on the lapel of her tweed jacket. Today's was a sea turtle, and she thought Megan would get a kick out of it since Harley had sent a toy turtle.

Evelyn entered the hospital through the main lobby, thinking she'd stop in and see Joy first. Joy was working a half day today in the gift shop. Anne was busy with her granddaughter, and Shirley was attending a women's event at church with her mother.

The lobby was slightly less crowded than on a weekday, but staff, patients, and visitors were crisscrossing the space on their various missions.

To her surprise, Evelyn recognized an older woman being pushed along in a wheelchair. It was Lavinia Snow, riding along with her handbag and jacket piled on her lap, her bandage-wrapped foot resting in front of her. She was also clutching a plastic bag given out by the hospital when they discharged patients.

What was she doing in here? Patients were usually discharged through a separate exit. Evelyn had her answer when she saw Lavinia pointing at the gift shop. The attendant veered the chair in that direction and as she did, Lavinia's handbag fell out of her lap and onto the lobby floor. Her wallet slid out. Lipstick rolled away. Comb and glasses case spilled. Evelyn rushed over to help.

"I'm sorry about that," the attendant said, bending down to scoop up Lavinia's wallet.

"It was my fault," Lavinia said. "I should have given you more warning."

Evelyn picked up the handbag, the green one Lavinia usually carried. As she did so, she noticed that a side seam had split. For such an expensive bag, it really wasn't well made.

She held the bag out to the attendant, who dropped Lavinia's things inside. "I hate to tell you this," Evelyn said. "But your bag is ripped." She showed Lavinia the tear.

"Oh no. That was a gift from my son." Lavinia reached out for the handbag, and Evelyn gave it to her. She examined the rip, frowning.

"All set," the attendant said, beginning to push the wheelchair along.

"How did your surgery go?" Evelyn fell into step beside the chair. She was going in that direction anyway.

Lavinia's frown relaxed as she glanced down at her foot. "It went very well, thank you. The surgeon was pleased, said I'd be dancing in no time." She laughed. "Imagine that. Me dancing."

"Why not?" the attendant put in. "Dancing is good for you, body and spirit."

"I have to agree with that," Evelyn said. She stepped back to allow Lavinia to be wheeled through the doorway.

"I'll be happy to wear my pretty shoes again." Lavinia's words drifted back to Evelyn. "My son gives me shoes as well as handbags, you know."

"That's nice, ma'am," the attendant said. "He sounds like a good son."

"He's the best." Lavinia's tone held a touch of smugness. "He takes good care of me."

Inside the gift shop, the attendant wheeled Lavinia to the magazine rack, where she glanced through the new issues. Evelyn went to say hello to Joy, who was behind the counter.

"Evelyn." Joy's face brightened. "I didn't expect to see you here today."

"I know," Evelyn said. "It's strange being here on my day off. But I wanted to pop up and see Megan."

Joy glanced at the clock. "If you can wait a few minutes, I'll go with you. Someone is coming to relieve me."

"I'd love that," Evelyn said. "Is that fresh coffee I smell?"

"Sure is." Joy pushed up her sleeves. "I'll get us a cup."

Evelyn's phone rang. Abigail. Her heart began to pound. Was she calling with good news? She moved away from the counter to answer. "Hello?"

"Evelyn? It's Abigail." The restaurant owner sounded bright and cheery, excited even. "I found Sabra's journal. Do you still want to read it?"

"Absolutely," Evelyn said. "I can't wait, actually."

"I have to go out later, so why don't I drop it off?" Abigail offered. "Where is a good place to meet?"

"I'm not working today, so my house would be best," Evelyn said. She gave Abigail the address. "What time do you think you'll be by? I'm out right now."

Abigail was silent for a beat. "How does one o'clock sound? Will that give you enough time to get home?"

"Plenty. See you then." What a treat. Evelyn couldn't wait to get her hands on the journal.

"What are you grinning about?" Joy asked, handing Evelyn a mug.

Evelyn took the coffee, lifting it in a salute of thanks. "I just had the best news. Abigail Gibbs Johnson found Sabra's journal. You know, Israel's daughter. Hopefully it will shed more light on Israel's life." She dropped her voice to a whisper. "And Benjamin's murder."

"Oh yes, I got your text about that last night. It's a real puzzler, isn't it?" Joy turned as Lavinia and the attendant approached the counter. "Are you all set?" she asked them. "I'll be right there."

While Joy checked Lavinia out, Evelyn browsed through the shop. Every time she came in, there was something new and fun. Today she found a cute little pin shaped like angel wings. She had to have it.

"Don't you love that pin?" Joy asked when she rang up Evelyn's purchase. "I bought a couple as stocking stuffers for Sabrina and the girls."

"Great idea." Evelyn tucked the pin into her purse. She would wear it in honor of the Angel of Mercy.

The gift shop volunteer showed up right then, so Evelyn and Joy left to go see Megan. On the way through the lobby, Evelyn saw Lavinia outside, being pushed toward a waiting vehicle.

A big black SUV, exactly like the one she had seen last night. And the one that had followed her and Anne two nights ago.

"Hold on," she said to Joy. "I'll be right back." She power walked across the lobby to the windows so she could get a better look.

But to her surprise, she saw Rufus, the security officer from the bank, jump down from the vehicle to help the discharged patient. What was he doing here at the hospital, picking up Lavinia? Maybe he had a job on the side as an Uber driver or chauffeur. Or maybe he was doing this as a favor for his boss. Mary Lou, the bank president's wife, and Lavinia were very good friends, after all.

Shaking her head, Evelyn hurried across the lobby to join Joy. "I'm sorry," she said. "I thought I was going to be able to put two and two together. But unfortunately not."

"It will all come together in due time," Joy said calmly. "How was your dinner at Abigail's last night?"

Evelyn filled her in on the way to the birthing center, concluding with Abigail's offer to let her read Sabra's journal. "She's bringing it by the house later. I can't wait to read it."

"I hope it has the missing pieces," Joy said. "But you've done an amazing job so far putting the story together."

"You think so?" Evelyn wasn't satisfied with her results, but it was nice to hear that her friends thought she was doing all right.

"I do," Joy said. "Think about it. You're trying to find out about events from over a hundred and fifty years ago. Too bad they didn't have social media back then. You know how social media lives forever."

Evelyn laughed. "Very true." She pictured how the events she was researching would look on social media, the posts and tweets and selfies. Oh my, that would be something.

There was a security guard posted outside the birthing center as usual. Recognizing them, he unlocked the door and let them in.

Evelyn couldn't help but think of Harley and how happy he would be when he met his son. He must be going crazy being separated from his family this way. But there were pretty powerful forces keeping them apart.

"I feel so bad for them both," Joy whispered as they made their way through the unit. "I can't even imagine what Megan is going through."

"Me neither." But Evelyn was glad that she and her friends could at least be supportive of the young mother. What if they hadn't met her, taken her under their wings so to speak? The poor thing would be sitting here in a strange city all alone.

"Good morning," Evelyn called out as they arrived at the room Megan had been using to care for Logan when she was on the unit.

Megan was cuddling little Logan in a front-facing carrier as she gazed out the window. "Hi, there. I'm so glad you came by." She turned toward the window again. "I was thinking about going outside."

"It's a good day for it," Evelyn said. "The temperature is already around eighty."

"Wow." Megan shook her head, her glossy hair swinging. "Up in Boston, it's thirty degrees. And it might snow, according to my mom."

"Do you want to go down to the garden?" Joy suggested. "It's really beautiful and restful. And if you're up for it, we can take a short walk along the waterfront."

Megan beamed. "They said I could do that, as long as I don't go far. And make sure to stay away from crowds." She stroked Logan's head, safely covered by a knit cap. "His immune system isn't ready for that yet."

"He looks bigger than he did yesterday," Evelyn said. "Can that be true?"

The young mother tilted her head back and forth, studying her son. "I think you're right."

"Take lots of pictures," Joy said. "Someday it will be hard to imagine that he was ever this small." She wandered over to the windows, where there were now four arrangements. "These are holding up pretty well."

"I've been pulling off dead blossoms and leaves to keep them fresh," Evelyn said. "And Shirley checked the water, what was it, yesterday?"

Joy, who couldn't keep her hands off flowers, began to fluff up the blossoms and even rearrange a couple. After tweaking one display, she turned it around so it showed to better advantage. Then she pulled back with a frown. "What is that?"

"What are you talking about?" Evelyn asked.

Joy pointed to a little square box attached to the side of the vase. "That doesn't belong there."

"Let me look." Evelyn strode over and bent close, grasping the little box with her fingernails. "It's stuck on."

Joy tugged at her sleeve, making Evelyn look up at her. "Stop," she mouthed. She put a finger to her lips before picking up the vase and carrying it into the bathroom. Then she came back out and shut the door.

"What was that all about?" Evelyn asked.

Joy took Evelyn's arm and urged her away from the bathroom door. Megan, who was gently rocking back and forth, her arms around Logan, watched in bemusement.

"I think it's a listening device," Joy whispered once all three women were standing close together. "It's exactly like the ones you see on TV. On those detective shows."

Chapter Nineteen

MEGAN'S HEAD JERKED UP. "A listening device?" A series of expressions—shock, confusion, and finally understanding—flowed over her face. "They must think I know where Harley is...that I'm protecting him."

We kind of are, Evelyn thought. But she didn't say the words out loud in case they could still be overheard somehow.

"You think Carson put it there?" Joy whispered.

"I think it's a strong possibility." Megan set her lips firmly. "Carson brought me a bouquet, which gave him the perfect way to leave it in here. Although I haven't said anything to him, Evelyn seeing him search the cottage with Preston's help told me one thing. He's not to be trusted. That was totally against protocol." She sighed. "I wish I dared call someone else at the FBI and ask them what's going on."

"Is there anyone else you can trust?" Joy asked.

"I'll give it some thought," Megan said. "It's so tricky. I thought I could trust Carson."

"Who are the other bouquets from?" Evelyn asked. She felt the need to be thorough, in case it wasn't the FBI agent who left the bug.

Megan studied the flowers still on the windowsill. "Well, you sent the one with roses, my parents gave me the sunflowers, and that one is from Carson."

Joy frowned. "So who sent the one I put in the bathroom?" Without waiting for an answer, she crossed the room and opened the bathroom door. A moment later she returned. "There isn't a signed card. But I recognize it as coming from the gift shop, even though I didn't sell it. One of the volunteers must have."

"Can you check the slips?" Evelyn asked. The room number was noted on those, often along with the patient name.

"Good idea," Joy said. "I'll pop in and do that when we leave here. It won't take long."

Evelyn turned to Megan. "Why don't we go out to the garden while Joy does that? And let's stop for sweet tea on the way."

A few minutes later, Evelyn and Megan were seated on a bench near the Angel of Mercy statue, sipping iced tea and enjoying the sunshine.

"I could get used to this," Megan said. "It feels like summer."

"The weather is wonderful here," Evelyn said. "Although New England is so pretty in the winter."

"Winter is pretty up there, yes," Megan said with a laugh. "But bone-chilling cold and way too long."

Evelyn slid a glance at her new friend. "You can always come back for a visit."

Megan adjusted Logan's cap. "Y'all are so nice. Logan and I really appreciate you." She laughed again. "See what I did there?"

"You're an official Southerner now," Evelyn said.

Megan dug out her phone then thought better of it. "Can I use your phone, Evelyn?" After Evelyn handed it over, she placed a call. "Hi, Mom. It's me, on a friend's phone. Sitting in the sunshine. Yes, it's eighty degrees here." Megan laughed. "Yeah, I know. Brr. Anyway,

Mom, have you heard from Harley? Has he called you?" Her face grew troubled. "I don't understand why he hasn't tried calling me."

Megan listened for a moment. "Yes, I had the same thought, which is why I'm on Evelyn's phone. Tell you what, Mom," she said, anger in her voice. "Once Harley shows up and is cleared, he's leaving the agency. He can take one of those consulting jobs they're always offering him. At least I won't have to worry where my husband is ever again."

Megan's mother spoke again, and although Evelyn couldn't hear her exact words, her tone was soothing. Megan gradually calmed down. "I know, Mom. Love you too. Oh, I'll send you a picture right now. We're sitting outside, next to an angel statue. Okay, I'll do that." She turned to Evelyn. "She wants a picture of me and Logan by the angel statue." But then her face fell. "But I really shouldn't share anything showing that we're in Charleston, should I, in case it gets out somehow?"

"Probably not," Evelyn said. "But I can take the picture and keep it for you. And how about a close-up? We'll send her that one for now."

As Megan stood in front of the Angel of Mercy, Logan in her arms, she said, "Mom thought my phone might be hacked. Or Harley thinks it is. That's why he hasn't called me."

"That makes sense," Evelyn said. Under normal circumstances, she might think such a conclusion was paranoia. But with the discovery of that odd little device in the room…well, Megan's line being hacked was definitely a possibility. Carson might even have warned the hospital switchboard to watch for Harley's call, in case he figured out Megan was in town.

Evelyn's stomach churned. She felt like she was living out one of those police television shows Joy had mentioned. But it wasn't as exciting as it appeared in fiction. As she took the photographs, she said a silent prayer that the Lord would send real angels to watch over mother and child.

After they returned to the bench, Evelyn showed Megan the pictures and texted the close-up for Megan to send to her mom. Then she asked, "Do you want us to keep looking for your husband?" Evelyn wanted to keep going but it was Megan's decision.

"Do you want to stop?" Megan's gaze was on her baby. She brushed her fingers across his soft cheek. "You've already done so much, I really can't ask you to do more."

"We don't want to stop," Evelyn said. "At least I don't. I'll have to check with the other ladies, see what they think, of course. But there's no harm in trying to track 'Lee' down, is there?" They could talk to Bryce and see if Lee had shown up again.

Megan's eyes grew teary. "Would you? Please? Otherwise I have no idea what's going on."

"All right, we will." Evelyn thought about possible next steps. "I'll let Bryce know that we'd like to talk to Lee. My assistant knows Bryce," she explained. "And I just had another idea. Why don't we get you one of those burner phones? Once we find him, we'll give Harley the number and he can call you on that instead of your regular cell."

"Good idea," Megan said. Her voice was pained. "Do you believe that I'm thinking this way? Hiding from my husband's boss? But at this point I don't know who to trust." She reached out and tapped Evelyn's forearm. "Except you and your friends."

Joy emerged through the lobby doors, glancing around for Evelyn and Megan. Spotting them, she made her way along the path to their bench.

"Any luck?" Evelyn asked, although she guessed by Joy's smile that she had been successful.

Megan moved over to make room on the bench. "It took me a few but yes, I found it. Like I thought, another clerk filled the order."

"Well, who was it?" Evelyn asked. "Don't torture us this way."

"Sorry," Joy said with a rueful smile. "Lavinia Snow sent the bouquet."

"Lavinia Snow?" Megan asked. "Harley was staying in her carriage house, right? I met her at the gift shop when she was at the hospital to have bunion surgery."

"That's her," Evelyn said. This turn of events raised another question. Had Lavinia made the connection between Megan Brooks and David Smith, her tenant? For a second she wondered if Lavinia had put the listening device on the flowers. But she hadn't been in the birthing unit, that Evelyn knew of, anyway, and the flowers had been delivered. So unless she put it on before the clerk sent it up... her brain hurt from all this speculation.

"This is really weird," Megan said. "Why would she do that?"

"I have no idea," Evelyn said. "Maybe she knows that your husband was working undercover. She didn't send flowers to all the new mothers, did she?" Thinking of another possibility, she bent forward so she could see Joy better. "Was there a mistake? Maybe Lavinia wanted to send the flowers to someone else."

"I thought of that too," Joy said. "But the order clearly said Mrs. Brooks, with the right room number."

With a sudden resolve, Evelyn rose to her feet. "Why don't we take that walk? Exercise always helps clear my mind."

Struggling to get up, Megan accepted Evelyn's hand with thanks. "I hope it clears mine. I'm totally confused."

"It will all work out," Joy proclaimed. She began to walk, pumping her fists. "Our prayers are being answered."

To Evelyn, Joy's words were a faith boost. As the trio—plus baby—began to stroll through the grounds, she loosened her shoulders and deliberately inhaled. Time to let her thoughts and worries go and enjoy the moment.

After the walk, during which they discussed the upcoming party for Logan, Evelyn and Joy escorted Megan back to the birthing center. A nurse looked up from the station when they walked in. "There you are, Mrs. Brooks. Someone was here looking for you."

Megan stopped in her tracks. "Really? Who?"

"A gentleman," the nurse said. "I didn't catch his name. He said he'd be right back."

"Can you hang around a few minutes?" Megan asked Evelyn and Joy after they reached the parenting room. She began to unfasten the baby carrier.

"Sure," Evelyn said. She popped into the bathroom to take a picture of the arrangement and a close-up of the odd device on its side. Maybe she and James could do some research and figure out exactly what it was.

The three friends waited in uneasy silence while Megan put a still sleeping Logan into his bassinet. Evelyn found herself clenching her fists tightly. What if, by some wild chance, it was Harley who had come to visit at last? Here to tell his wife that his mission was over and they could go home? Her heart twisted in hope and anguish.

But it wasn't Harley who knocked and hovered in the doorway. It was Carson Lewis. Evelyn found herself bristling, knowing that, after the FBI agent's actions at Harley's rental cottage, they couldn't trust him.

"Hey, Carson," Megan said in a listless voice.

Carson remained in the doorway, keeping his distance. "How are you, Megan? Ladies?" They murmured greetings in return. His gaze skimmed the flower arrangements, and when he frowned, Evelyn remembered the one with the bug was still in the bathroom. Purely to see his reaction, she went into the other room and retrieved it, then placed it near the others, pretending to fuss over it. Was it her imagination that his expression eased somewhat?

"Is there anything new concerning Harley?" Megan asked. "I'm very excited for him to meet his son."

"About that." Carson ran a hand through his perfect hair. "He's still missing. We've tried every avenue to get him to come in, but he's not responding."

"So you still think he's on the run." Megan's tone was flat. "A criminal."

Carson pressed his lips together. "I'm afraid so. But things would go better for him if he'd turn himself in." His brow furrowed in an expression of concern. "Surely you can see that, Megan." He moved farther into the room, pausing a short distance from where Logan slept.

"Not really." Megan folded her arms. "You mean he'd be arrested for a crime he didn't commit. There's no way he embezzled money from a bank."

Carson shook his head, but Evelyn couldn't tell if he was denying Megan's statement or implying that Harley was indeed guilty. He shifted around, echoing Megan's stance by crossing his arms. "Have you heard from him lately? Gotten a letter? Or a gift?"

Megan flinched at his questions. "No," she said slowly. "I haven't." Evelyn noticed what she did. She was speaking the truth, because it was Megan's mother who'd received Harley's latest postcard and gift.

The agent took a step into the room. "If you do, Megan, you need to call me right away. I'm serious. You don't want to be charged with obstruction of justice. Or aiding a fugitive."

The threats hit Evelyn like a blow. Would they really do that? Was she breaking the law as well? She glanced at Joy, who clasped her hands as if in prayer. No. Harley was innocent until proven guilty, right? Plus at the very least, he needed to speak for himself. They hadn't heard his side yet. And if he was guilty, well, then she would place the call herself. It would be her duty.

"You can threaten me all you want," Megan said without raising her voice. But Evelyn heard the ferocious roar of a mama bear underneath. "The fact remains that my husband is loyal to his country." She cocked her head. "In fact, I'm starting to wonder why he isn't coming in. I'm sure there's a very good reason."

She bent over the bassinet to arrange Logan's blanket, the stiff set of her back discouraging any further argument.

For an instant, a look of pure rage crossed Carson's face. But after noticing that Evelyn was staring at him, he rearranged his features into a semblance of compassion. "I'll chalk this discussion up to postpartum blues," he said, his tone oily. "I understand that women can be extra emotional at times like this. Think about it, Megan. Do the right thing." With that, he turned and strode out of the room.

Once he was safely gone, Megan growled and clenched her fists. "I'm so angry right now. I can't believe he actually threatened me. And then chalked up my valid concerns to postpartum depression."

"It's maddening," Joy said. "He's obviously trying to pressure you. We need to find Harley ourselves. And fast."

Chapter Twenty

EVELYN SAW THE TRUTH OF Joy's words. It was time to take action. "I'm going to make a couple of calls when I get home. I'll keep you both posted."

"And I'll be back by to drop off a phone for you, Megan," Joy said. While on their walk, Joy had offered to buy a throwaway phone when she went shopping that afternoon. "I'll text you the number, Evelyn."

"You two are the best," Megan said, hugging both women. She yawned, stretching both arms wide. "I'm exhausted. I think I'll take a nap." Her expression was rueful. "Before Logan wakes up."

Joy patted her shoulder. "Good plan. Getting rest is the most important thing you can do right now. Oh, and pray."

"Believe me, I've been praying," Megan said, her voice breaking. "Day and night."

"I know you have, darlin'." Joy embraced her again. "We're right there with you."

Evelyn and Joy said goodbye to Megan and Logan then walked out of the hospital together. They parted ways in front of the main gates. "I'm so glad you were here this morning," Evelyn said. "Your encouragement really keeps me going."

Joy threw her arms around Evelyn. "And your sheer dogged determination does the same for me. I admire you, Miss Evelyn."

"Right back atcha," Evelyn said, pleased by Joy's kind words. "Since you're going shopping, I'll send Anne and Shirley the updates, okay? I have nothing else on my agenda this afternoon but meeting with Abigail and making a few calls."

"I'll be in touch," Joy promised. With a wave, she set off down the sidewalk.

Back at the house, all was quiet. Evelyn let herself in and headed for the kitchen, where she made a sandwich and poured a glass of sweet tea. Since it was so nice out, she'd eat lunch on the balcony. And make her calls during lunch.

First Evelyn sent a text to Anne and Shirley, catching them up to speed. Then she sent a text to Stacia, asking if she was free to talk. Stacia wrote back immediately saying yes, so Evelyn called her.

"Hey, boss," Stacia said. Evelyn could hear music in the background. "What's up?"

"Where are you?" Evelyn asked, curious.

"I'm at the mall with a friend," came the answer. "She's in the dressing room, so I have a couple of minutes."

"I won't keep you long," Evelyn said. She got right to the point. "I need Bryce's phone number."

"Seriously?" Stacia's voice dipped. "I mean, why? Are you fixing him up with someone else? Because I strongly advise against that. If you like the person, that is."

"No, no, nothing like that," Evelyn said. There was no way around it. She was going to have to confide in her assistant. "A friend of mine asked me to look for a family member. We think he's living near the waterfront. And Bryce, well, long story short, he's seen the guy. So I want to talk to him again."

"Oh." The exclamation was long and drawn out. "I get it. It's one of your cases. Why didn't you say so?" She paused for a moment then recited Bryce's number. "Tell him I said hey. On second thought, scratch that." With a giggle, she signed off.

Stacia was the best, no doubt about it. Once everything was settled, Evelyn would fill her in. Evelyn sent Bryce a text asking if he'd seen the man he knew as Lee again, figuring he'd probably prefer that to a call.

Evelyn watched her phone while she ate the rest of her sandwich. No answer yet. Even though impatience was rampaging like wild horses in her veins, she'd give him a little longer. If need be, she'd go to his house—if Stacia had his address, that is—but she hoped it wouldn't come to that.

The doorbell rang, and Evelyn hurried downstairs to get it. When she opened the door, Abigail stood on the steps, her smile tentative. "I think I'm early," she said, shoulders rising in apology.

"No problem," Evelyn said. "Please come in. Would you like a glass of tea?"

"I'd love one." Abigail glanced around as she entered the house. "What a beautiful home."

"Thank you," Evelyn said, ushering her guest down the hall to the kitchen. "I grew up here, so lots of good memories."

"Just like Abigail's Kitchen." Abigail perched on a stool and opened her tote bag. "I've got the journal right here." She opened a manila envelope and pulled out a small, brown, leather-bound book.

Evelyn dispensed ice into two glasses then filled them with tea from the refrigerator. "Thanks for sharing. I can't wait to read it."

Abigail ran her fingers over the smooth cover. "I feel such a connection to my relatives now. Despite the struggle to get Israel recognized, I'm enjoying learning more about his life."

Evelyn handed her a glass then perched on an adjacent stool. "It wasn't short on excitement, that's for sure."

Her understatement surprised a laugh out of Abigail. She put a hand to her mouth. "You've got that right. Sure puts our troubles into perspective, doesn't it?"

"History has a way of doing that," Evelyn said. She thought about Israel's bravery in freeing enslaved people. "I can't see a man like Israel trying to rob someone or kill them. It doesn't add up." If Israel had wanted revenge, he certainly could have taken it during the chaotic raid.

"I totally agree." Abigail took a sip of tea, murmuring pleasure at its taste. "I can't thank you enough, Evelyn, for taking this on. I wouldn't know where to begin."

"Oh, it's not hard," Evelyn said. "But you have to refuse to take no for an answer. I ran into a couple of other dead ends too." Oops. Why had she said that? Not that she'd been meaning to hide anything from Abigail. But was now the time?

Apparently so, because Abigail said, "What were they?"

Time to come clean. Evelyn steeled herself. "I hate to tell you this, but Israel never got a military pension. And I couldn't find him listed as having served."

Abigail leaned back in her seat. "What? You've got to be kidding me. He was a veteran. Every Veterans Day we honor his service. Put flags on his grave and everything."

Evelyn winced. "I know. I didn't want to tell you this, believe me." And then the report of Benjamin's murder had overshadowed her concerns about Israel's military status. "But to put things into perspective, my husband, who is a history professor, says that historical records from that time were a mess. Even Harriet Tubman had trouble getting a pension. She had to fight for years. And she still didn't get her full due."

"That's not right," Abigail said. "That woman singlehandedly changed the course of history."

"And Israel helped," Evelyn said. "I'm so honored to help you get him recognized." Hopefully Sabra's journal would answer questions about the murder case, why Israel hadn't gone to jail or been executed.

"I'm grateful for your assistance." Abigail smiled brightly, seeming to shrug off her concerns. She pointed at Evelyn. "Oh, you know how I mentioned going to see Cora Beth to give her an update? We're going to have to wait until Monday. She had something come up this weekend."

"That will actually work better," Evelyn said. "I hope to make more progress this weekend." Her gaze fell on the vintage cookbook she'd been using for inspiration. "On another topic, what kind of dressing do you make on Thanksgiving?"

"Dressing?" Abigail picked up her iced tea. "Corn bread, of course."

After Abigail left, Evelyn curled up on a sofa with the journal. Inside the cover was written, *Sabra Gibbs, her journal. 1905. Reflections on a life*. The same year that Sabra had written up Israel's account of the raid. Perhaps doing that had triggered a desire to write down her own memories—and hopefully other stories about her parents.

She had barely turned the page when the phone rang. Hoping it was Bryce, she picked up. But the voice on the other end was that of a woman. "Evelyn? This is Patricia Cooper, over at the heritage society."

"Patricia, hello. I've been meaning to give you an update. We found the plantation records in Colleton County. And not only that, we found a letter from a general that proves Israel Gibbs went on the raid."

Patricia sucked in a breath. "That's wonderful. And guess what, Evelyn? I've got more for you about Israel and the raid."

"You do?" Evelyn flopped back, stunned by this good news. "Tell me, quick."

"I don't know if you noticed," Patricia went on, "but we have a book of oral histories put together early in the 1900s. A lot about the Civil War in there, naturally."

Evelyn had seen that book and had been intrigued by it. "Was Israel interviewed?"

"No, not Israel. But a man named Clement Snow was. He was a field hand on the Gibbs plantation. And a decorated Civil War veteran as well. He joined the Union Army after being freed."

There was that name again, Snow. The two families were certainly intertwined through history. "He knew Israel?" Evelyn held her breath, waiting for the answer.

"I'll say. He mentioned how Israel shared the good news that the raid was coming. And he saw Israel there that night, helping the enslaved escape. I get the sense that they were pretty close, because he mentions Israel encouraging him when they were in the hospital later on."

"Mercy Hospital?" Evelyn asked.

"Yes, that's right. You work there, don't you?"

"I do. Maybe I can find something in our records vault about their stay in the hospital. You won't believe what's in there." Evelyn laughed. "You'd probably love it."

"Oh, I would," Patricia said. "Just say the words 'old documents,' and I'm there." They shared a chuckle and then she said, "I can make a copy of Clement's oral history if you want, leave it here at the desk."

"How long are you open today?" Evelyn asked. "Maybe I'll come by and get them." She wouldn't have a car until James got home, which wouldn't be until dinnertime. But maybe Joy could run her over.

Patricia said she'd be onsite until five, so Evelyn told her she hoped to be there. Then she picked up the journal again, encouraged by their progress. With any luck, they would make Cora Beth's deadline with ease.

Chapter Twenty-One

"Thanks for coming to get me," Evelyn said as she slid into Joy's Mini Cooper. "It's really going to save me some time."

"No problem," Joy said, pulling away from the curb. "It worked out fine. After shopping, I swung by the hospital and gave Megan her new phone then headed over here." She glanced at Evelyn. "Anything new since I saw you?"

"Oh yes," Evelyn said. "I sent Bryce a text but haven't heard back yet. He's the young man who confirmed that Harley goes to a restaurant near the waterfront. I'm hoping Bryce can find out where he's staying."

"Me too," Joy said. "I'm about ready to do a house-to-house search for the man."

"I hope it doesn't come to that," Evelyn said, picturing them hitting the streets. "Besides getting a call from Patricia at the heritage society, I've been reading Sabra's journal." Even saying the words made Evelyn's stomach jump.

"What did you find out?" Joy's tone was knowing. "I can tell by your face that you've got news."

Evelyn laced her fingers together. "I do. I don't know everything yet, but the journal filled in quite a bit more of the story. Sabra was only a small child when everything happened, so she wrote down what her mother told her, she says." The murder wasn't a topic that Sabra wanted to discuss with her father, it seemed, probably because it was too painful.

"And?" Joy slowed as they approached a stop sign. "Go on. I'm dying over here."

"The newspaper accounts were right. Israel was accused of Benjamin's murder. After Belinda Gibbs identified him as the killer but before he could be arrested, friends spirited him out of the city. He didn't come back until after the war in 1865. The raid was in 1863, remember? He came back when his family got word to him that the charges were dropped. That had something to do with a walk Abigail took up and down Tradd Street."

Joy made an exclamation. "Not past Benjamin's house?"

"Yes." Once again, Evelyn was flooded with admiration for the brave young mother and wife. "She paraded the carriage back and forth, making sure to stop in front of the Gibbs house. She really took a risk. Not only was she goading the woman who had accused her husband of murder, Belinda and her household were stricken by yellow fever. It was bad in Charleston that year. Belinda died soon after."

"Did Belinda even see her?" Joy asked. She signaled a turn onto another street.

"Uh-huh. Belinda was on the second-floor veranda, lying on a chaise longue. I guess she wasn't too sick yet. Sabra said that at one point, her mother and Belinda locked eyes. Abigail knew Israel was innocent, and she could tell that Belinda knew it too. She was praying fervently the whole time, she told her daughter, that Belinda would do the right thing."

"Wow," Joy said. "What a dramatic story." She pulled up in front of the heritage society. "I'll wait here while you run in."

Evelyn put her hand on the door handle. "I'm so relieved that Israel wasn't tried for murder. But I have to admit being curious. Who shot Benjamin Gibbs, and why did Belinda lie about it?"

"Good question," Joy called.

Halfway up the steps to the society entrance, Evelyn's phone bleeped. Still moving, she pulled out her cell to see who had texted her.

Bryce. At last. Before going inside, Evelyn called him. From here, she saw Joy peering up at her, puzzled. Evelyn gave her a thumbs-up to tell her it was important.

"Yo," Bryce answered. From the background came the clatter of pool balls and voices.

"Bryce, it's Evelyn Perry. Thanks for getting back to me." She leaned up against the warm building wall to enjoy the sun.

"No prob. You said it's about Lee?"

"Yes. We really need to find him, talk to him. Have you seen him again?" She held her breath waiting for his answer.

"I haven't, but hey, hang on a minute." Bryce must have put his hand over the phone, because his voice was muffled speaking to someone. He came back on. "He's supposed to show up here this afternoon. For a pool tournament. Swing by if you can." He gave the time, which was half an hour from now.

"We'll do that," Evelyn promised. She was sure that Joy would want to go along. She could also take the opportunity to buy fresh oysters on the way back, which was perfect. "See you later." She put away her phone and hurried inside.

Patricia was at the desk. "You made it," she said, rising to her feet. She picked up an envelope and held it out. "Here it is. Enjoy."

Evelyn took the envelope. "Oh, I will. Thank you so much, Patricia. You've been a huge help. I hope you come to the exhibit when it opens."

"Wouldn't miss it." Patricia beamed with pleasure. "I love seeing all the pieces come together on a research project."

"So do I," Evelyn said fervently. "So do I." With a wave, she turned and rushed back through the doors. On to their next adventure.

"Who called?" Joy asked when Evelyn climbed into the Mini Cooper. "Oops, sorry. Didn't mean to be nosy."

"You're not," Evelyn said, putting on her seat belt. "It was Bryce. He said Harley should be showing up for a pool tournament this afternoon. Want to go?"

"Absolutely," Joy said, pulling out onto the street. "Think you should give Megan a call, tell her we've tracked down her husband?"

Evelyn thought about that. "I'd love to, but what if he doesn't show up? I'd hate to get her hopes up and then dash them like that."

"True. We'll wait then." Joy pressed the gas. "Give me directions, okay?"

They wove through the streets of the city then crossed the Ashley River on the westbound bridge, the same route Evelyn and Anne had taken to go to Colleton County. Soon they were pulling into the parking lot of A.J.'s, which was packed with pickup trucks, motorcycles, vans, and sedans.

"The pool tournament must be a big draw," Evelyn said. "There are a lot more people here."

"I guess so." Joy was able to squeeze the Mini into a tight space, one advantage of the compact car. "Lead on."

Inside, they paused for a moment in the entryway, taking in the scene. Most of the tables and booths were full, and there was a line at the counter.

"The pool tables are that way." Evelyn pointed. They made their way across the room, dodging around tables and avoiding people with trays.

Quite a crowd was gathered around the pool tables, with games underway at all three. Evelyn spotted Bryce laughing with another young man. To her surprise, she recognized Marvin, who worked at Abigail's Kitchen.

"Over there," Evelyn said to Joy before squeezing through the tight-packed bodies with murmurs of "Excuse me," and "I'm sorry."

Finally they arrived in front of Bryce. Evelyn greeted the two men. "Hey, Bryce. Marvin. How's it going?"

Bryce smiled, and Marvin said, "I know you. You're friends with my aunt."

"That's right, I am." Evelyn pulled Joy forward. "And this is Joy. Bryce, Marvin."

"Nice to meet you," Joy said. She glanced around. "Big crowd."

"Yeah, they all come out for the tournament," Marvin said. "It's a charity benefit for the food bank. Turkey boxes for needy families."

"That's so nice," Evelyn said. She would put some money in the donation jar on her way out.

"Abigail's Kitchen is one of the sponsors," Marvin said, pointing to a flyer taped to the wall. "We do pies and rolls."

"So Abigail sent you over to represent her?" Evelyn guessed.

Marvin laughed. "Yeah. Tough job but someone has to do it, right?"

Evelyn agreed then said to Bryce, "Is Lee here yet?"

"I don't think so." Bryce scanned the crowd. "No, I don't see him."

What if he didn't show up at all? "Do you know where he lives?" Evelyn asked.

"I don't," Bryce said. He shrugged. "Never came up."

"Yeah, you do," Marvin said. "Remember he told us? He's living on a boat. Fifty-footer, he said."

Bryce's mouth opened, and he nodded. "Oh, yeah, that does ring a bell."

"If you weren't so busy with the ladies, you might remember stuff," his friend teased.

"You mean he's docked at a marina?" Joy asked. By her frown, Evelyn knew what she was thinking. Marinas were pricy. Many of the yachts were worth more than her house.

"No, moored in the Ashley River," Marvin explained. "People do it all the time. No one bothers them if they stay out of the shipping lanes."

"Kind of like camping on a boat," Joy said. "I didn't know that."

If Harley was still on his mission, and Evelyn believed he was, then maybe a spot in the river gave him a good vantage point. With all the boats in Charleston, who would give one more a second look?

"We really need to talk to him," Evelyn said. "It's extremely urgent. Any idea how we can get hold of him?"

The two young men looked at each other. "We've got time before we play," Marvin said. "We can go down to the marina with you and see if he's there," he said to Evelyn. "He comes over in a dinghy then rides his motorcycle around town."

"Lead on," Evelyn said. Out in the parking lot, Bryce and Marvin hopped in Bryce's truck while Joy and Evelyn followed in the Mini. "This is exciting," Joy said. "I can't believe we're only minutes away from meeting Harley."

"I hear you," Evelyn said. She glanced at the street as they pulled out, alarmed when she saw a black SUV parked half a block down. Keeping her eyes on the vehicle, she went on. "We've heard so much about him, I feel like I know him."

"Same here." Joy glanced in her rearview mirror. "What are you looking at?"

Evelyn had craned her neck, still watching the SUV. It hadn't moved. "Nothing, I guess. Imagining things."

They followed the truck down a series of side streets, working their way toward the waterfront. This area of the city was mostly warehouses and small manufacturing companies. With a start, Evelyn recognized a business name on a sign: Lowcountry Imports. Preston Snow's company. His building was long, with loading bays along one end, Most were full, tractor-trailer trucks backed up to the big doors.

A couple of blocks later, they arrived at a small marina, the type that rented slips by the day and had a small, secured parking lot. Since parking cost money, Joy followed Bryce's lead and parked along the street. This time of year, many of the slips were empty. Most boaters dry-docked their crafts over the winter.

But there were always diehards, people who lived on their boats or chose to motor farther south after the holidays, to Florida or the Bahamas.

Bryce and Marvin waited for Evelyn and Joy to catch up, and then they walked into the marina, skirting around the closed gate. The sun was starting to sink in the west and its warm rays bathed the scene in golden light. The bay glittered, making Evelyn squint as she searched the water. There were a few cabin cruisers moored off shore. Was one of them Harley's?

"I don't see the dinghy," Bryce said. "And his motorcycle is still parked in the lot." He gestured to the parking area, where a few vehicles and motorcycles sat.

"What now?" Joy asked, the discouragement in her voice echoing the emotion Evelyn felt.

Marvin scanned the water. "He's still moored out there. See?" He pointed to a boat bobbing at anchor offshore.

"I have an idea," Bryce said. "Let's ask Bill to take them out." To Evelyn and Joy, he said, "Bill's in charge of security for the marina. Good guy."

"Yeah," Marvin said. "If Lee isn't coming in, they can go to him."

As they set off along the asphalt toward the floating docks, Joy asked Evelyn, "Ready for this?"

Evelyn smiled at her friend. "Why not? Taking a ride on the water wasn't in my plans, but at least it's warm today."

Soon they were on the docks proper, which bounced under their footsteps. Evelyn admired the boats still in the water as they passed by. Each sailboat and cabin cruiser was well-kept, cozy, and inviting.

Marvin stopped at a cabin cruiser moored at the very end. "Hey, Bill," he called. "You aboard?"

This boat was the exception that proved the rule. Although the deck was clean, the blue and white fiberglass was faded and the wheelhouse engines etched with salt.

"It's nicer than it looks," Bryce said, obviously reading Evelyn's expression. "He fixes up old boats and resells them for big money."

Marvin called out again, and the boat swayed as a man emerged from below. Bill was trim with a muscular physique. The US Marine Corps and American flags he had flying spoke to his service.

"Hey, boys. What's up?" His keen blue eyes skipped over Evelyn and Joy with curiosity.

Bryce introduced them then said, "They'd like to hitch a ride out to see Lee. They have a message from his family."

"It's urgent," Evelyn said. "And we'd really appreciate your help."

Bill's narrowed eyes flared briefly before he turned to study Lee's boat out in the channel. "I'll be glad to run you over."

"We won't take much of your time," Joy said.

The sailor took Joy's hand and helped her aboard. "No problem. I'm always glad to help someone out." He called to Bryce and Marvin. "Coming aboard?"

The young men conferred. "We really should head back for the tournament," Marvin said. "If that's okay?"

"That's fine," Evelyn said. "Thanks for your help. And I hope you do well today."

With a wave, the young men set off toward their vehicle.

"Ready, ladies?" Bill started the engine, and they were soon backing out of the slip.

Out on the water, in the moving boat, the breeze picked up. Evelyn turned up her collar to ward off the chill. To keep James informed, Evelyn sent him a text, including the boat registration number. She also mentioned that Bill was in charge of security for the marina, so he wouldn't worry.

"I like seeing Charleston from this angle," Joy said, sitting next to her on the bench seat. "Boat rides are so much fun."

"They are." But underneath the pleasure of skimming along, Evelyn's every nerve was tense with excitement. They were finally going to meet Harley. What perfect timing that Joy had a phone number he could safely use to call Megan.

Bill cut the engine as they approached Harley's boat. Evelyn could see him mopping the deck, dressed in casual work clothes, his hair tousled and the beginnings of a beard on his chin. A far cry from clean-cut banker David Smith.

Harley looked up as they drew closer, his face tense but blank. Likely seeing if they were friend or foe. Then he seemed to recognize Bill's boat and, after waving, he put the mop in the bucket and pushed it aside.

With expertise, Bill cut the engine so they glided close but didn't hit the other boat. Harley threw over a bumper attached to the rail so they could get closer.

"Hey, Lee," Bill called. "I have a couple of visitors for you." He wrapped a line around a cleat to connect the two boats.

Harley's eyes swept over Evelyn and Joy, confusion in his expression. He glanced toward shore and then back. "It's really not a good time right—"

"We know Megan," Evelyn said quickly.

An expression of surprise ran over Harley's features, followed by curiosity. "I can take it from here, Bill," he said. "I'll run them back."

"Good enough," Bill replied. He and Harley helped the women make the transfer to the other boat. Then he backed up and motored away.

"Okay, ladies, what's going on?" Harley asked. "How do you know my wife?"

Evelyn looked at Joy. Where to begin? "She's in Charleston," Evelyn said. "She came here looking for you."

Harley ran a hand through his hair. Then he gave them a rueful smile. "She did, huh? I guess I should have expected something like that. But I really thought everything would be wrapped up here way before now." He set his jaw. "We had some…um, complications." Then he frowned. "How did you find me? And why did she send you? Where is she exactly?"

Once again, Evelyn looked at Joy, who nodded, encouraging her to take the lead. "It's a long story, but the most important part is, your son arrived early," she said. "Logan is his name. He's fine. She's fine. They're at Mercy Hospital, where we work. That's how we met her. And we know everything. Well, most of it."

Again, Harley's face showed confusion but then he grinned. "A son? I have a son?"

"You do," Joy said. "And he's beautiful."

Harley's hand went to his pocket and he pulled out his phone. Then he shook his head. "The worst part of this whole thing is, I haven't been able to call Megan. Even on this phone, which is a burner. I'm afraid her calls are being monitored."

"We were worried about that too," Joy said. "So we got her a burner phone. And we have the number."

His eyes lit up. "Awesome. What is it?" As Joy recited the number, he punched them into his phone.

"Go ahead and call her," Evelyn said. "She's dying to hear from you."

"I'll do that." Harley indicated a leather bench seat. "But first, where are my manners? Please, have a seat. Do either of you want something cold to drink?" He opened a cooler. "I have water and iced tea."

"Water, please," Evelyn said, settling next to Joy, who echoed her request. "I can't tell you how excited we are to finally meet you, Harley. We've been looking for you for a few days now."

He twisted the tops on two bottles and handed them over. "I'm glad it was you who found me. After things went south at the bank, I had to lay low."

"That's what we figured." Sensing his impatience, Evelyn said, "Go on and call her. We're happy to wait."

He stepped down into the boat's cabin, and soon they heard the murmur of his voice.

"Oh, Evelyn," Joy said, "this is wonderful. I'm so glad we finally found him."

"Me too," Evelyn said. "I can't wait until they can reunite in person." Hopefully that would be soon, once Harley's mission wrapped up.

"Whoa, look at that," Joy said, pointing to a cigarette boat racing across the water. "He's going way too fast." The boat held two men, both wearing sunglasses.

"He sure is." Then Evelyn's pulse leaped. "They're coming right toward us."

Harley ran up from below, the phone still in his hand, and stared at the approaching craft. "Uh-oh. Looks like we've got company."

Chapter Twenty-Two

Harley was now on full alert, his persona of vagabond sailor shed like a cloak. "I'm not expecting anyone right now, so this is not good." He made a shooing motion to Evelyn and Joy. "Quick. You two need to go below."

Without argument, Evelyn and Joy clambered down a ladder into the cabin. The surprisingly spacious room had a galley kitchen and dining area with banquettes. A couple of doors led to sleeping quarters and bathroom, Evelyn guessed.

"Who do you suppose it is?" Joy whispered. The cigarette boat's engine was audible even down here, growing louder as it came closer.

"I have a good idea," Evelyn said. Her heart was hammering, every instinct telling her to hide. But instead she put a finger to her lips and crept back up the ladder.

Joy tugged on her jacket hem. "What are you doing, Evelyn?"

"I want to see what's going on." Evelyn peeked out of the bulkhead, noticing that she had a good view of the deck while still sheltered from visibility. "Come on up. There's room for you."

With a groan, Joy climbed up again and, squeezing together, they shared a rung close to the top.

The cigarette boat cut its engine and pulled up alongside. Evelyn couldn't see it from here, but the men's voices were clearly heard.

"Harley Brooks, I do declare," one man said. "Or should I call you David Smith?"

"See? I told you he was out here," another said.

"That's Carson Lewis," Evelyn whispered, recognizing his voice.

"Oh no." Joy said. "How did Carson find him?"

Evelyn groaned, thinking of the black SUV she'd spotted near the restaurant. "I think we led him here by accident. He's not one of the good guys."

"I don't think so either," Joy said. "I don't trust him a bit."

Joy's voice had risen, so Evelyn hushed her again. She glanced around. What could they do to help Harley? She moved up the ladder onto the deck, staying low to remain out of sight. Joy grumbled but a moment later was right beside her.

Harley was standing at the railing, talking to Carson and Buford Martin. "If you know what's good for you, you'll get out of here," he said. "Not that I should be warning you."

Carson gave a scoffing laugh. "You're under arrest, Harley Brooks, for embezzlement."

"Wouldn't it be a shame if Carson's gun went off?" Buford asked with a chuckle. "I can see the headline now. 'Agent resists arrest.'"

"I should be arresting you, Carson," Harley said. "That embezzling charge won't hold water. But the money laundering one will stick. And a whole list of others."

"You don't know anything," Carson snarled.

Harley's hands slowly rose, and he stepped back. But still he warned, "I didn't welcome you aboard. You're trespassing."

"So what?" Carson's head and shoulders appeared at the rear ladder, and he grabbed the side of the boat, ready to boost himself over the railing.

Evelyn's glance fell on the bucket and mop standing nearby. Acting on impulse, she picked up the bucket and sloshed the soapy water in an arc that completely soaked Carson and caused him to lose his grip.

Then Joy got into the act. Grabbing the mop, she ran forward and pushed the soapy tangle of strings right into Carson's face. He shouted again and fell backward, landing in the water with a huge splash.

A moment later he bobbed to the surface. "Help me, why don't you?" Carson snarled at Buford, who had let the cigarette boat drift away a short distance. "Throw me that life ring."

Joy elbowed Evelyn. "We sure make a good team."

Evelyn slung an arm around her friend's shoulders. "Yes, we do."

"Great job, ladies." Harley ran to the controls. "Hang on. We're out of here." The boat engine started with a roar, and they set off across the water.

Behind them, Buford was still trying to help Carson climb up into the cigarette boat. This wasn't an easy task, because the boat kept drifting.

"I take it that Carson is actually the rogue agent," Evelyn said. "He tried to tell us that you were."

Harley's lips set in a grim line. "That figures. When I found money missing in some of the accounts under my control, I knew I was being set up. I was there to look into Lowcountry Imports, but these were other accounts."

"He's probably the one who bugged Megan's room," Evelyn said, thinking that the agent had put the device on another vase, not his own, because that was too obvious. "And followed us around in a big black SUV. I spotted him several times over the past few days."

Joy's mouth opened. "My goodness. That man is as crooked as a dog's hind leg." That was one of her colorful Texas sayings.

"You got that right." Harley's marine radio squawked, and he reached for the microphone. "I'm heading in now," he said in response to a message that was cryptic to Evelyn's ears. "Might want to send someone to pick up a couple of clowns." He recited the cigarette boat's hull registration number. "Carson Lewis and Buford Martin. Subjects are armed." The other person said something. "Yeah, that's right. Intel said they're supposed to be meeting Snow at the warehouse. But they showed up here first."

So Carson was working with Preston Snow, as they had thought. Evelyn glanced at the cigarette boat, which was now a distance away. Carson, drenched and dripping, was now inside and by his gestures, she could tell he was shouting at Buford. He patted under his arm—a common spot for a holster—then looked inside his jacket. Oops. He must have lost something when he fell into the water. It was on the bottom of the river now.

"Not anymore," Evelyn said. "I think he lost his gun."

Harley glanced over his shoulder. "Couldn't happen to a nicer guy. But I'll let the information stand, just in case."

Over on the bridge, a convoy of police cars and emergency vehicles raced along toward the west shore, lights flashing.

"What's going on?" Joy asked. "It looks serious."

Harley grinned. "Oh, a little something I put into motion. They're about to raid a certain business. Big sting is going down." He sighed. "Months of work and, finally, success."

"Lowcountry Imports," Evelyn said.

He gave her a look of surprise. "How do you know that?" His eyes narrowed. "Who are you, really?"

"She's our brilliant friend," Joy said. "Give her a puzzle, and in five minutes she'll figure it all out."

Evelyn shrugged coolly, but she was thrilled by their compliments. "In addition to banking at Charleston City Trust, Preston Snow is a very good friend of Buford's. But we saw them arguing after you disappeared. And then I watched as Carson and Preston searched the carriage house you rented. That didn't seem right to me, that the FBI would involve a civilian in an investigation. Megan confirmed that Carson was wrong to let Preston help."

"And she was right," Harley said. "Chain of custody would be all messed up."

The emergency vehicles had crossed the bridge and were moving swiftly toward Lowcountry's warehouse, which was visible from the water. Judging by the lack of movement around the facility, no one inside seemed to have caught on yet.

Why would they raid the warehouse if the case involved money laundering? Two more pieces of the puzzle popped into Evelyn's mind. Lavinia's ugly green pocketbook. The knockoffs in the Savannah raid. "Are they importing knockoffs?" she asked.

Intent on bringing the boat into shore, Harley only spared her a glance. "Right again. Now tell me, Evelyn, how did you figure that out?"

"Lavinia Snow's handbag," she said crisply. "It looks like an expensive designer bag, but it's really poorly made. A few days ago, I saw a news story about a knockoff smuggling ring in Georgia. Are the two connected?"

"They absolutely are," Harley said. "And that raid helped us build a case here in Charleston. Companies are bringing in containers of fraudulent goods while creating invoices that reflect designer prices. That's how they're hiding the money that Buford's bank is moving offshore."

Whenever Evelyn heard about complicated criminal activity, she wondered how much lawbreakers could achieve if they used their powers for good.

"But keep it quiet for now, okay?" Harley urged. "Once this raid hits the news you can talk all you want."

Under Harley's direction, Evelyn and Joy helped him secure the cabin cruiser when they reached the marina docks. "I've got to run," Harley said. "Will you be all right from here?"

"My car is parked outside the gate, so yes," Joy said.

Harley began to trot along the dock. Then he turned and began to run backward, his charming grin breaking across his face. He gave them two thumbs-up. "I can never thank you two enough. You're my angels of mercy."

As he turned again, Evelyn said, "Did you hear that? Do you think he said it on purpose, thinking of our statue?"

"Maybe," Joy said. "But either way I'm tickled. We certainly did our good deed for the day, my friend."

"I'll say." Evelyn released a huge sigh. "I'm so happy we found Harley and that he's okay." She took Joy's hand. "Let's say a prayer of gratitude."

The two women bent their heads to thank God for this answered prayer. Then they began walking along the dock again, eager to get home.

Out in the river, a marine patrol boat was chasing the cigarette boat, which was now zooming north. Evelyn had a feeling they wouldn't get far. Over at Lowcountry's warehouse, blue and white lights were flashing. The raid was underway.

As they set off in Joy's car, Evelyn asked, "Do you mind if we make one more stop?"

"As long as it doesn't involve a boat ride and fending off criminals," Joy said with a laugh.

"Far from it," Evelyn said. "Although my husband might think my planned recipe is a crime. I want to pick up some fresh oysters."

"For the dressing you mentioned?" Joy asked. "You'll have to tell me how it turns out."

"I will. And after James decides which new one he likes best, I'll make it for Thanksgiving, along with the corn bread dressing." It probably wouldn't be the one with prunes, she guessed.

That evening, Evelyn brought James up to date over grilled red grouper, which went perfectly with the oyster dressing.

"Tell me again how you found him?" he asked. "Talk about a trail of bread crumbs. Tiny little clues."

"I know." Evelyn marveled at how one piece of information had led to another. "I have to believe God was guiding my steps. Isn't He wonderful?"

James smiled at his wife. "He is, indeed."

Evelyn's phone chimed with a notification. She usually didn't look at it during meals but today was an exception. "It's hit the news," she said. "Federal agents raided Lowcountry and made a number of arrests."

"So what's next for my Evie?" James asked. "Besides hosting Thanksgiving dinner."

Evelyn pointed her fork at him. "You're on carving duty, don't forget."

"Don't worry, I'll be sharpening knives in my lair," James joked. "How many do we have coming?"

"Hmm. Let me think." Evelyn counted quickly. "Ten plus us, so twelve. Oh, maybe we should invite Megan and Harley, make it an even fourteen, if they're still around."

"Will they still be in Charleston, do you think?" James asked.

"I don't know," Evelyn said. "It depends on when they release Logan. He's making good progress, but Megan said there are still a couple of issues they're watching." She felt a pang of sadness. "I really don't want them to leave, which I suppose is selfish of me."

"You've gotten close to Megan," James said. "So it's totally understandable."

"Nothing like a relationship forged in adversity," Evelyn said. She thought back to the day they'd met Megan, in distress because her husband had vanished.

James set his fork down and dabbed his mouth with a napkin. "That was delish."

"Even the oyster dressing?" Evelyn asked.

"Especially the oyster dressing. If you want to make it for Thanksgiving, I'm good with that."

Decision made. They rose and began to clear the table.

"Dessert in the study?" he asked. "We can catch the news. Find out more about the raid, hopefully."

"Sounds good," Evelyn said. "Ice cream okay?"

A few minutes later they were settled in front of the television, watching Bailey Carver report the raid on Lowcountry Imports. Containers full of knockoff goods from overseas had been discovered as well. Along with employees and managers, Preston Snow had been arrested, Bailey said.

A picture of Buford Martin flashed onto the screen. "Also caught up in this sweep was Buford Martin, president of Charleston City Trust," Bailey said. "It's alleged that Lowcountry Imports was laundering money through accounts at City Trust, with the bank president's knowledge."

"No mention of Carson Lewis," Evelyn noted. "Maybe that will come out later."

"Probably," James said. "No doubt he'll be indicted at some point."

Evelyn's heart went out to Mary Lou, Buford's wife. Maybe she'd known about his criminal activities, in which case sympathy wasn't needed. But what if she hadn't? Such a proud descendant of a founding Charleston family must be mortified.

Her phone began to blow up as Anne, Joy, Shirley, and Megan all called her. "I guess the news is out."

"Sounds like it." James levered himself from the armchair. "I'll go get us iced tea."

Working quickly, Evelyn put them on conference, grateful her phone allowed five people at a time. "Hey, y'all. We're all set."

"Did you see the news about Lowcountry Imports?" Anne asked in excitement.

"Sure did." Joy's voice was bubbly. "Evelyn and I were right there when it all went down, as they say."

"Get out of here," Shirley said. "Seriously?"

"Yes, we were, actually," Evelyn said. "But before we tell you about it, I want to ask Megan a question. Have you seen Harley?"

"Not yet," Megan said. "But oh, it was so wonderful to talk to him." She sounded as though she were over the moon. "He's coming to the hospital tonight. I can't *wait* for him to meet Logan."

The other women chimed in with exclamations of joy. "And we can't wait to meet your husband," Anne said. "Those of us who haven't had the honor, that is." She had a teasing tone in her voice.

"You'll have plenty of opportunities," Megan said. "As of tonight, he's on leave."

"That's wonderful," Evelyn said. She went on, with Joy's help, to fill them in on the afternoon's events. They all got quite a kick out of the story, especially the part involving the bucket of soapy water and the mop.

Shirley's hearty laugh rang out. "Oh my. Is that what you call a mopping-up operation, Joy?"

They all laughed.

"While I have you," Evelyn said once they had thoroughly hashed over the event, "are we all set for Logan's welcome party?" They were having the party on Veterans Day, a holiday for Evelyn. A community room in the birthing center had been reserved.

"Can Harley come?" Megan asked. Her question was met with a chorus of assent.

After going over the plan, everyone got ready to sign off. Then Shirley said, "Evelyn, before we hang up, did you find out anything more about Israel?"

Her question required Evelyn to switch gears and talk about what she'd read earlier in Sabra's journal, how the unfair charges against Israel had been dropped. Had it only been hours ago? It felt like weeks. James, who had returned to the study, listened in with interest. "There are still a few holes regarding the murder case," Evelyn concluded. "But I think we have enough for Cora Beth to add Israel to the exhibit." She thought of the envelope holding Clement Snow's oral history. She hadn't even had a chance to read it yet.

"Excellent," Shirley said. "I'm so happy to hear that."

"Me too," Evelyn said, smiling at James. "It sure was a challenge." As she said goodbye to her friends, she wondered if they would ever know the rest of the story.

Chapter Twenty-Three

"Oh, this is beautiful." Megan stood in the doorway of the community room, both hands to her face. Right behind her was Harley, clean-shaven and with a fresh haircut, holding Logan in a carrier.

"I'm so glad you like it." Evelyn beamed with pleasure as the couple took in the balloons, flowers, wrapped gifts, and the elaborate cake sitting in pride of place. Anne had worked for hours making and decorating the green-and-white-frosted cake topped with booties, a toy turtle, and a Boston Red Sox pennant. The last was a nod to Megan's hometown.

In addition to the gifts for Logan, the ladies had made another stack, the beginnings of a Caring Closet, one of Joy's brainstorms. The Caring Closet would provide necessary items for needy new mothers who gave birth at Mercy. Megan had made one of their first cash donations.

Anne guided Megan and Harley to seats at the head of the table, where she handed them glittery headbands that read, Mom, and Dad. Logan got a new cap that read, Rock Star.

"Glass of punch?" Joy asked, poised to ladle the fruity drink into small glass cups.

"I'd love one," Harley said, setting Logan's carrier down between their chairs. "A friend told me the South was known for its hospitality." He accepted the drink with thanks. "I'll be sure to tell him he was right."

Shirley slid spoons into bowls of potato and pasta salad. "This is ready whenever people want to eat." Besides the salads, there were finger sandwiches, veggie platters, and chips.

"It looks great," Anne said, stealing a potato chip and giving it to Addie, her granddaughter. "People should start arriving any minute." The gathering was small, with only the friends and their families—and Stacia. Regina, Shirley's mother, was already there and admiring the baby, but soon Joy's daughter and her granddaughters arrived.

Evelyn gave a few words of welcome. "Thanks for coming today," she said. "As most of you know, Megan was visiting Charleston when Logan made his unexpected and early arrival." The baby happened to squeak right then, which made everyone laugh. "Thankfully she was right here at the hospital when she went into labor. Shirley whisked her off to the emergency room, and then she was sent here to the birthing center, where we have the best team in the South." Everyone clapped. "Help yourselves to lunch, and then we'll get started." Evelyn stood back to let the guests line up at the food table.

Harley got up to load plates for himself and Megan. "This is fantastic, Evelyn," he said. "Thanks again for all you and your friends have done."

"We're happy we could help," Evelyn said. Lowering her voice, she said, "Is there any more news about the case?"

Harley nodded. "I'll share what I can after the party. If you have time."

"I need to leave by three, so yes, I have plenty of time." Evelyn was planning to help Abigail decorate Israel's grave, official veteran or not. Joy had made a spectacular bouquet that Evelyn was delivering.

During lunch, Joy led the group in a couple of funny games, and then it was time for gifts and cake. "We're going to need a truck to carry all this back to Boston," Megan joked. "It'll never fit in my suitcase."

"Speaking of which," Harley said. "We have an announcement." Silence fell over the room. "I'm leaving the agency, something Megan has wanted for a while. I have a lead on a job in South Carolina. But the clincher is, Megan's parents have decided to retire down here next year. Megan's mom is doing better, thankfully."

Megan beamed. "I'd love to live in the South, but I was worried about leaving my parents. Now I don't have to." She threw her arms around her husband. "I love you, Harley Brooks."

The whole room said, "Aww," before bursting into joyous laughter. A startled Logan began to cry. Megan scooped him up, rocking him in her arms while Harley unwrapped the rest of the gifts. The women teased him about how careful he was not to rip the paper, unlike Megan, who tore into them.

"I take great pride in my work," he retorted, folding the paper.

Megan smiled proudly. "He sure does. That's how he brought down a huge criminal operation."

"I suppose Buford Martin will be resigning from the hospital board," Joy said. "If he hasn't already."

"I can't help but feel sorry for Mary Lou." Regina's voice cut through the chatter. "She's done so much for charity in this city." Others chimed in, giving examples of Mary Lou's generosity.

Regina's kind words struck Evelyn's heart. She'd wondered about Mary Lou as well. Maybe she should call on her and see how she was doing.

Once the gifts were unwrapped, Joy's daughter and grandchildren left after expressing well wishes to the young couple. Evelyn and her friends, including Regina and Stacia, were the only ones left.

"We still have this room for another half hour," Anne said. "So no hurry."

"That will give us time to clean up," Shirley said, making up plates of leftover food to take to hospital employees. She was taking the rest of the cake to the main break room, where it would be quickly demolished.

Harley put his arm around Megan, who was still holding Logan. "I want to thank you all for stepping in to help my wife. She certainly was put in an awkward predicament, one of the main reasons I'm leaving law enforcement." He kissed the top of her head. "I never want anything like that to happen again."

"What exactly did happen?" Evelyn asked. "We know bits and pieces but that's all."

Harley sighed. "I took this assignment because another agent had a car accident and was out. It was supposed to be temporary, only a few weeks. Carson's reaction was the first indication that something was wrong. He was on vacation when I was assigned, and he went ballistic."

"Carson went to college in South Carolina," Megan said. "I didn't know that until recently."

"So he's friends with Buford and Preston?" Anne asked.

Harley nodded. "He'd done his best to stall agency efforts all along. But when the investigation in Georgia broke, evidence indicated that Lowcountry Imports was involved."

Evelyn remembered seeing the Georgia story on the news. "So Buford did his best to get rid of you," Evelyn guessed. "By framing you for embezzlement."

"Exactly," Harley said. "I happened to uncover some irregularities one day in the accounts I managed. That, along with a couple of offhand comments Buford made, told me he knew exactly who I was. So I left for lunch, got my stuff out of the carriage house, and never went back."

"You left your volcano paperweight behind," Megan said. "And Evelyn saw it on your desk, so it helped us find you."

"That's right," Evelyn said. "I guessed it was personal rather than belonging to the bank. And as far as I know, it's still sitting there."

"Maybe someone can pick it up for you," Megan said. "Unless they send you in again as part of the wrap-up."

Harley's face was rueful. "They might. But a whole lot of people are probably going to be angry with me. The bank probably isn't going to survive."

"Not your fault," Evelyn said. "Besides, Rufus thought the world of you. I'm sure the other employees did too."

"Ah, Rufus," Harley said. "Good man." He looked at his wife. "Do you have the stuffed turtle I sent you?"

Megan looked surprised at this change of topic, but she said, "Yes, right here." She pulled it out of Logan's diaper bag and handed it to him. Then she gasped as Harley pulled out a tiny Swiss Army knife and began cutting the turtle's belly seam. "What are you doing?"

"You'll see." He dug around in the stuffing and pulled out a small, slim thumb drive. "My backup evidence. Just in case." He didn't need to elaborate.

Evelyn looked at the other women and they all laughed. "We had no idea."

"I know one thing," Megan said. "I know God guided you into that gift shop, Harley. Because you bought the card and turtle there, I met these ladies."

"Amen," Joy said. "He sure did."

"And I'm eternally grateful," Harley said. He returned to his story. "Despite having to leave the bank so abruptly, I wasn't about to drop the case. So I went even deeper undercover and started working with the Coast Guard and Customs. They've been trying to stop the import of knockoff goods for a while. Lowcountry Imports was running the operation, the bank funneled money to offshore accounts, and Carson ran interference to keep it off the radar. Carson even used Buford's vehicle to follow you, Evelyn. He thought you might recognize a government vehicle. He said he wanted to intimidate you, without letting you know it was him."

"Well, it worked," Evelyn said. "Being tailed was creepy. Though I didn't let it stop me."

"I bet it was," Harley said. "Carson, Preston, and Buford will all be going away for a while. They're still trying to figure out if the agent I replaced played a role as well."

"Speaking of smuggled goods, do you remember Lavinia's handbag?" Evelyn asked the others. "The poor quality really tipped me off that it was a knockoff."

"I didn't like the color," Anne said. "But I have pretty simple taste. Certainly not designer."

"The other agencies set me up with a boat and a new name," Harley went on. "I hung around the docks, working as a casual laborer. That helped me get the lay of the land."

"And you went to A.J.'s and made some new friends," Evelyn said. She turned to Stacia. "Bryce helped us find Harley. He knew where his boat was moored."

Stacia rolled her eyes. "I'm glad he was good for something." Everyone laughed.

"Oh," Joy said. "The listening device on the vase. Was it Carson's?"

Harley's brow furrowed. "Yes. Though he put it on someone else's arrangement, not his own, of course, to throw people off if they noticed."

Which had worked. They thought that Lavinia might have placed it there, since it was on her flowers. And they still didn't know why she had sent a bouquet to Megan, she realized.

"Plus he hacked Megan's phone, we've discovered," Harley was saying. He pulled his wife closer. "I had the feeling he'd pull that, so I didn't dare contact you."

"That's what I thought might happen," Megan said. "I knew you hadn't abandoned us. Even though Carson tried to make me think you had."

"I'd never abandon you, babe." Harley's voice was husky. He reached out a finger and touched Logan's cheek. "Or this little guy either."

Evelyn was sure that Carson's ears must be burning, wherever he was. But he certainly had been unkind to Megan. She thought of another question. "Lavinia Snow sent Megan a bouquet. I've been wondering why. She met you in the gift shop, Megan, but you didn't give your last name."

Megan nodded. "That's right, I didn't, on purpose."

"I have an answer to that," Harley said. "Lavinia is a nice woman who had no idea what her son was up to. Not until recently, that is. Her husband always took care of the business, and she was content to let Preston take over when he died. But during the interviews we've conducted with her, she said she overheard Carson and Preston talking about me after I left the bank and the carriage house."

He grimaced. "I did give her a clue about you, Megan, inadvertently. She popped by to see me one day and saw a picture of you on my laptop. A recent one. I'd been using a virtual private network, one that was totally secure, so I took a peek at your social media. Left the page up by accident. Rookie mistake."

"That must be why she recognized me in the gift shop," Megan said. "Remember, ladies? It was pretty shocking at the time." Understanding dawned. "She must have noticed I wasn't pregnant anymore. But how—"

Harley sighed. "Carson. He was trying to find out if Lavinia knew anything about my whereabouts. He must have been desperate when he tried to use the news about the baby as leverage."

"Poor Lavinia," Joy said. "What a position to be in."

"So sending me flowers was an attempt to say she was sorry," Megan said.

"Or maybe to give someone a hint that she knew the truth," Evelyn said. "Probably both," she added upon reflection. "I'm glad we're getting all the loose ends wrapped up. But on another topic, where are y'all going to be for Thanksgiving?"

Harley and Megan exchanged looks. "We're not totally sure," Megan said. "Logan will probably be discharged by then, but they haven't given us a final date. He needs to put on some more weight and meet a few development milestones."

"If you aren't back in Boston by then, do you want to come to my house for Thanksgiving?" Evelyn asked. "I'm hosting the gang this year."

"What a nice invitation," Harley said. "What do you think, Megan?"

"I think we'd love to come," Megan said. "If we're still here. I can't think of a more appropriate holiday to celebrate with you all." She smiled down at her baby. "I'm certainly full of thanksgiving this year."

A few small groups were scattered about the Mother Emmanuel graveyard, adorning graves or standing together in prayer. Evelyn spotted Abigail in a far corner, on her knees trimming grass around a simple gray headstone.

"They do a nice job here," Abigail said as Evelyn walked up. "But I like to groom right around the stone." Rising to her feet, she noticed the bouquet in Evelyn's arms. "Wow, that's gorgeous."

"Isn't it?" Evelyn said as she placed the urn where Abigail indicated. "Joy made it. Most of the flowers came from her garden."

"It's extra special, then." Abigail clasped her hands together, and the pair stood in silence for a moment, honoring Israel's service.

"I have something for you," Evelyn said after Abigail signaled she was finished. She dug around in her bag and pulled out a copy of Clement Snow's story. "Patricia Cooper at the heritage society found an oral history that mentions Israel." As Abigail leafed through the pages, she added, "I marked the passages for you." Clement had considered Israel, "the finest man I know," and a "real hero."

Abigail read the account. "This is amazing," she said after she finished. "Can you go with me to see Cora Beth? As I told you, she's working today despite the holiday." The curator was taking advantage of a slow day to finish the exhibit.

"Sure can." Evelyn pulled out another envelope part way. It held the documents Abigail needed to prove Israel's participation in the raid. "I have another surprise for you." She pushed the envelope back inside and took hold of a smaller one. "I finally got into the archives and guess what I found?" Evelyn heard the thrill in her own voice. She'd been so excited with her success that she'd shouted, to Stacia's amusement.

Abigail took the manila envelope and unfastened the tabs. Inside was a photograph showing two handsome, elderly men sitting together near the Angel of Mercy statue. Both wore big smiles. "There's my gramps," she said. "And who is that with him?"

"Clement," Evelyn said. "Both men spent time in the hospital, and someone happened to snap a picture. That copy is for you. I also have one for Cora Beth, for the exhibit."

"Awesome," Abigail said. "I have his wedding portrait but that's it. People back then didn't take selfies every minute." She laughed.

Evelyn laughed too. "I kind of wish they had. We'd have much more complete records of their lives, wouldn't we?"

"We sure would." Abigail straightened a small flag she'd pressed into the soil. "I'm ready if you are."

Evelyn had the car, and she followed Abigail's vehicle over to Tradd Street, where they parked in front of the Ezekiel Snow House. The sign on the door said CLOSED, but as Cora Beth had instructed, they walked inside anyway.

"Cora Beth?" Abigail called as they crossed the hushed entrance hall. None of the overhead lights were on, so the room was dim and shadowed.

"I'm in here," the curator called from the main room.

Evelyn and Abigail found her taking a framed picture down from the wall. "We brought the information you requested," Evelyn said, suppressing her glee. Cora Beth had given them a deadline and they had more than met it.

Cora Beth turned with a smile. "I thought as much," she said as she leaned the picture against the wall. "That's why I'm making room."

Abigail's eyes were like stars. "I can't believe it's really happening. I'm so proud of Israel, I could burst."

"As you should be." Evelyn opened her tote and pulled out an envelope for Cora Beth. "Not only did we find a Union Army general's letter mentioning Israel as one of Harriet Tubman's scouts, we found an eyewitness account."

Cora Beth gave a little gasp. "An eyewitness account? That is downright amazing."

"It was a real stroke of luck, I have to admit," Evelyn said, not wanting to take unearned credit. "Patricia Cooper found it in

Clement Snow's oral history. He was one of the enslaved people Israel helped free during the raid."

Cora Beth took the envelope. "You can't get more eyewitness than that."

"Show her the real pièce de résistance," Abigail urged.

Evelyn dug for the second envelope marked with Cora Beth's name. "I happened to find a picture of Israel and Clement in the hospital archives. They were both patients there at the same time."

After setting aside the larger envelope, Cora Beth opened the smaller and pulled out the photo. "This is perfect," she said. "I'll slide it into a frame and it will go right here, beside Israel's story." She held it up in the newly blank spot on the wall.

"I can't wait to see the exhibit when it's all done," Abigail said. "I'm bringing everyone I know to the opening. And that's a lot of folks."

"Please do," Cora Beth said. "We're also going to feature it online. Plus I've had inquiries from schools for private group showings. By the time we're done, everyone in South Carolina is going to know about our brave men and women."

"And probably beyond the state too," Evelyn said. "I'm sure the online exhibit will get a lot of clicks."

"I hope so," Cora Beth said. "The more impact we have, the easier it is to raise donations." A troubled expression crossed her face. "The Snows gave us a huge endowment, which is still fine, but with recent events…"

Evelyn guessed she was referring to Preston Snow's arrest and the effect that might have on the museum's reputation. The Snows had donated the Ezekiel Snow House, which an ancestor had owned, so there would always be a known connection. "All you can do is keep moving forward," she said. "No matter what obstacles you face." She diverted the topic slightly. "The way I had to when the microfilm was missing."

Cora Beth seized on the change of subject. "That was strange. Did Patricia ever figure out where it went?"

Evelyn shook her head. "I don't think so. But it doesn't matter now, not for this project. We have all we need." There were a few more questions, though, ones Cora Beth couldn't answer. But maybe the woman down the street could. And should.

"Are you ready?" Evelyn asked Abigail as she hitched the tote strap over her shoulder. "I have one more stop to make, if you'd like to come along."

The Benjamin Gibbs House looked as forlorn and dark as the museum. "Do you think she's home?" Abigail asked, her voice a whisper. They'd left their cars parked and walked up the street.

"Maybe not, but let's see." Evelyn opened the gate and walked along the path through the silent garden. She wouldn't be surprised to learn that Mary Lou had fled the city after her husband's arrest. What a scandal, especially for someone who prided herself on her family history and standing in the community.

With Abigail at her side, Evelyn knocked on the door glass then rang the bell. After a moment, she heard shuffling footsteps beyond the door, and soon the door was cracked open to reveal a disheveled Mary Lou. One side of her hair was sticking up, her lipstick was crooked, and she was wearing ratty old slippers. She was a far cry from the immaculate, controlled matron Evelyn had first met.

"Can we come in?" Evelyn asked in a soft voice. "We won't stay long."

"We?" Mary Lou peered beyond Evelyn and took in Abigail.

"This is Abigail Gibbs Johnson," Evelyn said. "She's a descendant of Israel Gibbs."

In response, Mary Lou opened the door wide and stepped back. Then she turned and shuffled toward the parlor, leaving her guests to follow. Abigail took in the mansion with wide eyes, craning her neck as she went.

"I don't think they've changed a thing since 1863," Evelyn whispered. That brought a smile to Abigail's face, as she'd hoped.

"Have a seat," Mary Lou said. She'd already flopped down on a sofa in front of the fireplace.

Evelyn chose an armchair, as did Abigail. An uneasy silence fell over the room. Mary Lou toyed with the silk fringe on a pillow while her guests stared at each other.

Finally Evelyn cleared her throat. "I'm really sorry for your trouble, Mary Lou." And she was, sorry that Mary Lou's husband was a crook and this proud woman had to suffer the consequences.

Without lifting her eyes from the pillow, Mary Lou flapped a hand. "I'll be okay, I guess. At least I still have my home." Now her eyes went up, taking in the high ceiling with its ornate plasterwork. "Somehow we Gibbses managed to hang on to the place."

"As did we," Abigail said. "Oh, it wasn't as elegant as this, but Abigail's Kitchen was and still is our family business."

Mary Lou's face softened. "And you make the best fried chicken in town." She sat up more. "Maybe I'll come by and get a plate soon." She put a hand to her midriff. "I haven't been able to eat the last few days."

Evelyn understood, since she also couldn't eat while under stress. "Besides checking on you, Mary Lou, I have a couple of questions." Now Evelyn's stomach knotted up. Their hostess might throw them out once she realized why they were here. "They concern Israel. Well, Benjamin's murder, actually."

Mary Lou set her lips firmly, as if she'd expected this inquiry. She rose to her feet and went to the fireplace, where she began to arrange objects on the mantel. "Go on," she said, standing with her back to the room.

"Through my research and with the help of an ancestor's journal, Abigail and I found out about the murder of Benjamin Gibbs. Right here in this house." Evelyn had shared the contents of Sabra's journal with Abigail already.

"He was shot in cold blood in the entrance hall. On the stairs, actually. He fell down and landed, stone cold dead." Mary Lou's voice was flat.

"That's what I read," Evelyn said. "And at first his wife, Belinda, told the police that Israel was guilty. But Israel left town before he could be arrested. And then later, when he returned, he was told the charges were dropped."

Mary Lou didn't say anything for a long moment. "So it all worked out. What is it you want to know?"

"Who broke in that night, Mary Lou?"

Their hostess rested both hands on the mantel, her head bent as she stared into the empty fireplace. Finally she spoke, her voice hoarse and dry as if the words pained her. "Belinda shot the intruder. She never knew his name. By his ragged uniform, she guessed he was a deserter, thinking he could make an easy score."

Evelyn wondered if her expression was as stunned as Abigail's. It was one thing to have a theory, quite another to hear it validated.

Mary Lou whirled around to face them, folding her arms. "She buried the man under the oak tree, with the help of a servant."

"That's why you never cut down the tree," Evelyn said. "Even though it's on its last legs." Mary Lou nodded agreement.

"So why did she say Israel did it?" Abigail was both shocked and angry.

"She was out of her mind," Mary Lou said. "The war. Losing the plantation. Now her husband was killed right in front of her eyes." At Abigail's exclamation, she put up a hand. "I suppose to Belinda, who had lost so much, blaming Israel allowed her to get some sort of revenge. Of course it also got her off the hook for shooting a man. Even though it was self-defense."

"But she had a change of heart," Evelyn said. "After she saw Israel's wife."

Mary Lou returned to the sofa, collapsing as if boneless. "Yes, she did. She was quite sick with yellow fever, and she thought she'd better right a wrong." The twist of her lips was wry. "Although she never went so far as to admit killing the soldier. She wrote a letter to the police, recanting her accusation. She told them she'd made a mistake. That's the story passed down through my family, anyway."

"One more thing," Evelyn said. "Did you take the microfilm from the heritage society?"

Mary Lou nodded, her expression sheepish. "I knew I couldn't stop you from learning the truth. But I hoped I could slow you down a little."

"None of this has to be made public," Evelyn said. "We got what we wanted, Israel's recognition for his role in the raid." Maybe if she were a different sort of person, she'd shout the truth far and wide. But it was up to Mary Lou and Abigail, since the incident had affected their families.

"Thank you for your honesty," Abigail said with a sigh of relief. "It's good to know the whole story. And no, I don't plan to talk about the murder. I'm happy that Israel was cleared, that's all."

"One more thing," Evelyn said, wanting to tie up all the loose ends. "The oak tree. Maybe it's time to put those old bones to rest as well."

Mary Lou was toying with the pillow again. Now she set it in the corner, arranging it just so. "Maybe." Her face crumpled. "It's not as if I have any reputation left at this point." Putting both hands over her face, she burst into tears. "How could Buford do that? He's a huge criminal, and I had no idea." Her voice rose to a wail.

Moving in unison, Evelyn and Abigail joined Mary Lou on the couch, one on each side. "Hang in there," Evelyn said. "I think you'll find that most people understand. The ones who count, anyway."

Abigail handed her a clean tissue. "Come by Abigail's Kitchen anytime, Mary Lou. We'll do right by you."

"Everyone speaks of your big heart and generosity," Evelyn added. "Keep on being you, Mary Lou. It will all work out."

Mary Lou dabbed at her eyes. "You think? I do love my charity work." She sniffled. "Maybe I won't have as much money, but I can give my time, right?"

"We all offer what we can," Evelyn said. Gathering up her nerve, she decided to imitate her friend Joy for a moment. "Why don't we say a little prayer before we go? Ask God for His help and guidance."

The three women joined hands and bowed their heads. Evelyn led the prayer, firmly believing that many blessings were ahead for Mary Lou. She also prayed for Buford and the Snows, knowing that God's redeeming hand was at work.

Mary Lou was crying again, but her face was radiant. She hugged Evelyn and Abigail in turn. "Thank you, friends," she said. "You've given me new hope."

Not for the first time, Evelyn was humbled by the Lord's goodness. Not only had she helped reunite a family, she had helped a deserving hero win recognition. And now, like the cherry topping a sundae, she was able to support a grieving woman who needed a fresh start. She thought of a favorite verse from Psalm 107. "'Let them give thanks to the Lord for his unfailing love and his wonderful deeds,'" she whispered. "Thank You, Lord."

Chapter Twenty-Four

EVELYN ROSE EARLY ON THANKSGIVING Day, leaving James still snoozing. She had a twenty-five-pound turkey to get into the oven and two kinds of dressing to make.

Down in the kitchen, she puttered about, making coffee first of course then hefting the big bird out of the fridge. Logan had been discharged on Monday, but Megan and Harley had decided to stay in Charleston for the week. Megan's parents had come down, and with the addition of Curtis and Donna, the group had grown to sixteen people. In addition to generous helpings, Evelyn liked to have some leftover turkey for sandwiches and soups.

Evelyn made a rub with olive oil and herbs and covered every inch of the turkey. The giblets and liver went into a pan to simmer, forming the basis for rich gravy. The oven beeped and she slid in the pan, grateful that the turkey actually fit. Once the dressings were made, she had ten pounds of potatoes to peel.

Joy was first to arrive, and with Evelyn's help, she brought in several bouquets for the table and her casseroles. These were already cooked and would be warmed up later, in Evelyn's second oven.

While Joy perched on a stool with coffee, Evelyn got out ingredients for the dressings. Oysters. Cornmeal. Dry bread. Spices.

"What was the final verdict on dressing?" Joy asked.

"Oyster and corn bread," Evelyn said, grabbing a sauté pan. "Taste-test approved by James."

"Oh yes, I remember the taste tests. From when I had dinner with you." Joy smiled. "If you give me a knife and a cutting board, I'll dice onions and celery."

They were in the thick of chopping and dicing, sautéing and stirring when Anne, Ralph, and Addie showed up, pies in hand. Pumpkin, apple, and chocolate chess, made the traditional way from family recipes.

"Coffee is ready," Evelyn said. "And Addie, I can whip up some hot chocolate for you."

Addie gazed up at her grandmother. "Yes, please!"

Anne tapped her on the nose. "Then we're going to help set the table."

"James will be down to put in the leaves," Evelyn said. "Ralph, want to help him? We have sixteen eating today."

"I'll be happy to help," Ralph answered.

"Wow," Addie said. "Is sixteen a lot of people?"

They all laughed. "The short answer is yes," Joy said. "But working together makes it much easier."

"Baby Logan is coming too," Anne told her granddaughter. "Along with his parents and grandparents. Remember him?"

"Yay," Addie said. "Oh, he's so cute." The doorbell rang. "I'll get it." She bolted out of the kitchen.

Shirley and Regina joined them, Regina toting a bag of biscuit ingredients while Shirley held the corn casserole. "The biscuits need to be made fresh," Regina said. "I like to serve them hot with lots of butter."

"We can do that," Evelyn said. "I have two ovens." She grabbed her notebook and reached for a pencil. "I'll need to do a schedule though. We've got casseroles to heat and the biscuits to bake. After the dressings are done."

Her friends exchanged looks. "Oh, Evelyn, I was so glad you wanted to host," Anne said. "Only you could coordinate a meal this size so well."

The others clapped and Evelyn took a mock bow, her cheeks burning. "Well, as Psalm 107 says, 'He satisfies the thirsty and fills the hungry with good things.' Just trying to do my part."

Joy put down the paring knife and wiped her hands. "Okay, everyone. Before we go any further, group prayer. We've got a lot to be thankful for this year."

Addie's eyes shone. "I'm thankful for baby Logan."

"We all are," Anne said, pulling her close. "He and his mother were surely surrounded by mercy."

"Literally," Evelyn said. They all laughed.

Dear Reader,

Welcome back to beautiful Charleston, South Carolina, for this entry in the fabulous Sweet Carolina Mysteries series. I now live in New England (again), but I spent eight glorious years in the South. Charleston is truly a jewel, with its historic buildings, coastal location, and deep history.

I was especially excited when I was assigned to write a book featuring Evelyn. Like Evelyn, I am a history buff. Nothing intrigues me more than digging into a mystery from the past. While developing the plot, I came across a little-known event in Civil War history—the Combahee River Raid, led by Harriet Tubman. I just had to include this wonderful, heroic story in my historical thread! I talk more about the raid in this book's The Story Behind the Story.

While writing, I loved my virtual visit to Charleston in November, which is much nicer weather-wise than where I am now. It's also great fun to include a holiday, so of course Evelyn and the gang celebrate Thanksgiving—and most importantly, talk about the menu. I've featured a very traditional Southern Thanksgiving dish: corn bread dressing, recipe included.

I sincerely hope you enjoyed *Surrounded by Mercy*, and thanks for reading.

Signed,

Elizabeth Penney

About the Author

ELIZABETH PENNEY IS THE AUTHOR of more than two dozen novels for Guideposts, St. Martin's Press, and Annie's Fiction. She is a member of Sisters in Crime and the owner of a writing company, 2 Penney Productions. A former consultant and nonprofit executive, Elizabeth grew up in Maine and now lives in the White Mountains of New Hampshire, where she pens novels and tries to grow things. Visit elizabethpenneyauthor.com to learn more about Elizabeth's work.

The Story Behind the Story

MOST PEOPLE ARE FAMILIAR WITH Harriet Tubman's work in the Underground Railroad, which helped enslaved people escape from the South through a network of transportation routes and safe houses. But not as many know about her critical role in another exploit that freed over seven hundred men, women, and children—in one night.

Besides guiding enslaved people north, Harriet also worked with the Union Army as a spy and scout, often in the covert roles of nurse or cook. Indeed, she had served in both roles on the plantation since she was a child. Although she was formerly enslaved herself and it put her in danger of recapture, she covertly returned to the South time and again, saving the lives of many enslaved men, women, and children, giving them a future and a hope. A devoutly religious woman, she trusted in God every step of the way.

In the spring of 1863, the Union Army began making forays into the Low Country near Charleston, South Carolina, to obtain supplies and destroy plantations. Rivers were also full of mines set by the Confederate Army, and those needed to be cleared. Harriet Tubman and a band of river pilots, who knew the waterways well, were invaluable in helping Colonel James Montgomery map the area in advance.

Colonel Montgomery had a great deal of respect and admiration for Harriet, and he asked her to help lead a raid into the very heart of plantation country. Three gunboats, three hundred soldiers, and Harriet and her band of scouts sailed up the Combahee River late on June 1, 1863. She helped guide the boats up the tidal river, past land mines and with knowledge of where Confederate troops were stationed. All through the night they worked their way up the river. Although one boat ran aground, they continued to forge ahead.

Word had been given in advance to the enslaved men and women about the raid, and they were ready and waiting. Plantation after plantation, newly freed men and women exclaimed in joy and thanksgiving as they were carried to freedom.

This exciting and pivotal event is beginning to get the attention it deserves. It's been included in television and film productions and is the subject of a forthcoming book by Dr. Edda Fields-Black, Associate Professor at Carnegie Mellon University. Hearing a presentation by Dr. Fields-Black helped me enormously in writing this book. She also answered questions for me. Isaac Gibbs is fictional, but the outcome of his story is not. Dr. Fields-Black told me that none of Harriet's scouts received a military pension for their role in this raid for whatever reason, so not much is known about them. I hope they too get the recognition they deserve for their bravery.

Good for What Ails You

Evelyn's Corn Bread Dressing

Corn bread dressing is a Southern classic, and like her mother and grandmother before her, Evelyn makes it every Thanksgiving. It's a favorite with friends and family, especially James, her husband. Oh, and by the way, in the South it's called dressing, not stuffing, because it's baked separately instead of inside the turkey.

There are two steps to this recipe. The first is making a batch of corn bread—without sugar. Then the crumbled corn bread is added to the soup mixture, spooned into a pan, and baked.

Cornbread Ingredients:

- 1½ cups milk
- 2 tablespoons cider vinegar
- 1½ cups cornmeal
- ½ cup flour
- 1 tablespoon baking powder
- 1 teaspoon salt
- 2 tablespoons butter
- ¼ cup butter
- 1 egg
- ½ teaspoon baking soda

Casserole Ingredients:

- 1 cup onion, finely diced
- 1 cup celery, finely diced
- 3–4 tablespoons butter
- 1 (10.75 ounce) can of cream of chicken soup
- 1 (10.75 ounce) can of cream of celery soup
- 1 (14.5 ounce) can of chicken broth
- ½ teaspoon pepper
- 1 teaspoon dried sage

Directions:

1. Preheat oven to 450 degrees.
2. To 1½ cups milk, add two tablespoons cider vinegar. Mix and put aside. (alternative: 1½ cups buttermilk)
3. In a bowl, whisk together 1½ cups cornmeal, ½ cup flour, 1 tablespoon baking powder, and 1 teaspoon salt.
4. When oven is preheated, melt 2 tablespoons butter in ten-inch cast iron skillet on stove. Melt ¼ cup butter in microwave.
5. Gently whisk one egg and ½ teaspoon of baking soda into milk. Fold into dry ingredients with spatula. Mixture will be lumpy.
6. Once butter sizzles, add ¼ cup butter to batter, stir, and pour into pan. Cook for one minute.
7. Put skillet into oven for 20 to 25 minutes, or until corn bread is golden brown.
8. Cool.

Put together the corn bread dressing.

9. Sauté onion and celery in butter on stovetop until soft.
10. Crumble corn bread into small pieces in large bowl.

11. Add sautéed vegetables, cream soups, chicken broth, pepper, and dried sage. Mix thoroughly.
12. Press into greased 9×13 pan, cook at 350 degrees for 30 to 40 minutes until golden brown and set.

Serve with roasted turkey, chicken, or ham.

Read on for a sneak peek of another exciting book in the Sweet Carolina Mysteries series!

Broken Bonds
BY DeANNA JULIE DODSON

Joy Atkins drained the last of the coffee from her mug and looked around the Mercy Hospital gift shop with satisfaction. She had restocked the shelves and tidied up in general. She'd also arranged the potted poinsettias on a series of boxes in one corner so they made what looked like a leafy red and green Christmas tree. It was only ten days until Christmas, and one could never have too many flowers.

Right after Thanksgiving, she had put up the lights and garlands and ornaments that made the shop twinkle and glimmer like Santa's workshop. But now she thought a little something new was in order. The poinsettia tree was the perfect thing.

She glanced at her watch and smiled. "I'm leaving now, Lacy," she called to the volunteer who took over for her until the shop closed. "See you soon."

"I'll be right out," Lacy called back from the shop's storage room. "You go ahead."

"Thanks. See you tomorrow."

December weather in Charleston wasn't generally cold. It had been in the low sixties all day, but it had also been rainy and windy, so Joy had brought a light jacket with her to the shop. She stuffed her arms into it, snatched up her purse, and headed toward the door, looking down as she buttoned up. Two steps later she ran straight into the person coming into the shop.

"Miss Joy?"

Joy frowned, for an instant not recognizing the tall young man in front of her. Then she broke into a smile and pulled him into her arms.

"Chris! Oh, my goodness, Chris Breck! What are you doing here? Is your mother with you?" She looked him up and down. "I almost didn't recognize you."

"I guess the last time you saw me was when I graduated from high school before Mom and I moved to Dallas. I've got only one semester of college left now."

She reached up and pushed a thick lock of wavy black hair away from his forehead, seeing in his face his mother's dark eyes and his father's determined jaw. But she saw, too, a puffiness in his face, especially around his eyes.

"How are you, Chris?" she said, taking his arm. "How's your mother? I've been meaning to call her."

"She wanted me to tell you she's been meaning to call you," he said with the mischievous grin she remembered too well, but the grin quickly faded. "She said to tell you again how sorry she is that she couldn't come see you when Mr. Wilson died. You were with us when Dad had his heart attack."

"I told her it was all right. She can't help it if she was sick. It just happened that way. And we talked on the phone a lot back then. That was what I needed most anyway. Just to talk. We both understood what it meant to lose a husband."

"She's wanted to come see you since, but the company she works for is restructuring and she can't get away right now. I guess we all get busy. And it looks like I caught you at a bad time."

"No, of course not. Not a bad time, just the time when I usually go home. What did you have in mind?"

"Uh, do you think you have a minute to talk to me?"

"Of course." She studied his face again. "Chris, is something wrong?"

He shrugged. "I came because Mom said—"

He broke off when Lacy came out of the storeroom and a couple of young girls came into the shop.

"Can we talk someplace?" he asked, lowering his voice.

"We can go to the coffee shop. Nobody will bother us there."

He smiled tentatively. "That'd be great. I'll buy."

"Oh no. You're the guest."

She clasped his arm a little more tightly and guided him out the door and into the hospital lobby. This was the old part of the hospital, a lovely mix of old and new under a blue-sky painted ceiling. The dangling cut-crystal of the antique gas lamp caught the light from the lavish decorations and scattered the multicolored reflection like jewels across the white marble floor.

Chris smiled as he looked up at it, red, green, and gold dancing in his eyes. "It's sure Christmas in here."

"Pretty, isn't it?"

She was glad to see that the coffee shop was empty except for a middle-aged couple. She got coffee and Chris got bottled water, and they sat down on the opposite side of the room.

"Tell me what's wrong," she said when he didn't speak first. "Are you sure your mother's okay?"

She and Kathy Tallwater, now Breck, had known each other from the time Kathy's family moved in next door when Joy was in the fifth grade. Joy had been Kathy's babysitter for a while, and later, despite their five-year age difference, they had grown to be friends. Kathy's husband died right after Chris got out of high school, and she and her family had moved to Dallas. They had kept in touch, but it had been awhile, probably since Kathy's birthday in July, since they'd actually had time to talk.

"Mom's fine," Chris said.

Joy studied his face again. "What about you, Chris?"

Several months ago, Kathy had mentioned that he was having some problems, but she said it wasn't anything the doctors would have trouble treating. Seeing him now, Joy wasn't so sure.

He looked down at his bottled water. "Knowing Mom, she already told you I've been having some kidney issues."

"It sounded like it wasn't anything major."

"We didn't think so at first. Now…now I need a transplant."

"Oh, Chris." She put her hand over his. "I'm so sorry."

He smiled faintly. "It's going to be all right. I think so anyway. But that's not what I came to talk to you about."

She waited for him to go on.

"I was going to get a kidney from my cousin Peter, my dad's sister's son. We did all the preliminary tests to see if we were compatible, and Pete was all ready to do it, but then we found out we weren't a match."

"That's too bad."

"It wasn't only that," Chris said. "We found out we're not related at all."

Joy blinked at him. "What?"

"That's what I said. But it gets better. When I found that out about Pete, we did DNA tests for his mother too, and it turns out I'm not related to her either. And I'm not related to her and Dad's parents."

"This is crazy. Are you saying you think you were adopted?"

He laughed half under his breath. "That would be the easy answer, right?"

"There's no way," Joy said. "I remember when your mom found out she was expecting you. I was at the hospital when you were born."

"But that's not what's in question anyway. I'm definitely related to my mom and my dad, but I'm not related to my grandparents. The ones on Dad's side anyway."

Joy could only shake her head in disbelief. "You mean your dad was adopted and he didn't know it?"

"Not according to his parents. And I've seen pictures of my grandmother when she was expecting him and when he was in the hospital and when they brought him home. I believe my grandparents when they say he was their son, their own flesh and blood. I just don't know how it could be."

"Maybe there was some kind of problem with the testing," Joy suggested.

Chris shook his head. "I had it done twice, each time by a different company. Same results."

"I don't know what to tell you, honey. Is there something I can do to help?"

"Yeah," he said. "I found out from my grandmother that Dad was born in this hospital. When Mom heard that, she told me I should come see you."

"You realize I work in the gift shop, don't you?"

"I know, but I thought maybe you'd know some way I can check into Dad's records here. I don't know, maybe somebody's files got messed up and he got switched with somebody else."

Joy chuckled. "That would be very unlikely. Doctors and nurses are very careful when a baby is born. They immediately take footprints and handprints and put on an ID bracelet."

"I know," Chris said. "I mean, I know it's supposed to work that way, but what if it didn't? What if there was like a one-in-a-million sequence of errors and a mix-up really did happen?"

"Okay, say that's possible. Does it make any difference now? I mean, your dad was still your dad, wasn't he?"

"I know, but here's the deal—I don't have any relatives on Mom's side of the family. Yeah, I'm on a list to get a transplant, but who knows when they'll find a match for me? I thought if I could find my dad's family, I mean, his biological family, maybe one of them would be a match."

"And maybe they'd be willing to give you a kidney?" Joy asked with the lift of one eyebrow.

"It's worth a try, isn't it? Can't you just help me find out?"

He looked at her with those big brown eyes that had gotten him his way from the time he was tiny, and as always, she couldn't resist.

"All right," she said finally. "I have a friend who works in the records department. Maybe she can give us more information."

"Great." He downed the rest of his water. "Can we go talk to her now?"

"I suppose so. I know she's working today. But you're going to have to get permission to see those records."

"Sure." He took a piece of paper from his wallet. "This is from my grandmother. It gives me permission to look at her medical records here when she had my dad."

Joy studied the note. "Well, that seems in order." She took another sip of her drink and then stood up. "I can't promise you anything, okay? But we can certainly go ask."

"It's worth a try," he said with a hopeful grin.

She put her arm through his again. "You haven't changed since you were five years old."

It was nice to hear him laugh.